BUILDINGS & LANDSCAPES

JOURNAL OF THE VERNACULAR ARCHITECTURE FORUM
VOLUME 31 | NUMBER 1 | SPRING 2024

Buildings & Landscapes (ISSN 1936-0886) is published twice a year in the spring and fall by the University of Minnesota Press, 111 Third Avenue South, Suite 290, Minneapolis, MN 55401-2520. http://www.upress.umn.edu.

Published in cooperation with the Vernacular Architecture Forum (VAF). Members of the VAF receive the journal as one of the benefits of membership. For further information about membership, go to http://www.vernaculararchitectureforum.org/join.

Copyright 2024 by the Vernacular Architecture Forum

All rights reserved. With the exception of fair use, no part of this publication may be reproduced, stored in a retrieval system, or transmitted, in any form or by any means, electronic, mechanical, photocopying, recording, or otherwise, without a license or authorization from the Copyright Clearance Center (CCC) or the prior written permission of the Vernacular Architecture Forum.

Postmaster: Send address changes to *Buildings & Landscapes,* University of Minnesota Press, 111 Third Avenue South, Suite 290, Minneapolis, MN 55401-2520.

Manuscripts should be prepared to conform to the *Chicago Manual of Style.* Contributors agree that manuscripts submitted to *Buildings & Landscapes* will not be submitted for publication elsewhere while under review by the journal. Please feel free to direct any inquiries to either editor: Michael J. Chiarappa, Washington College, Center for Environment and Society, 485 South Cross Street, Chestertown, Maryland 21620, mchiarappa2@washcoll.edu; Margaret M. Grubiak, Department of Humanities, Villanova University, 800 E. Lancaster Avenue, Villanova, Pennsylvania 19085, margaret.grubiak@villanova.edu. Please see https://vafweb.org/buildingsandlandscapes for author guidelines.

Address subscription orders, changes of address, and business correspondence (including requests for permission and advertising orders) to *Buildings & Landscapes,* University of Minnesota Press, 111 Third Avenue South, Suite 290, Minneapolis, MN 55401–2520.

Subscriptions: For our current subscription rates please see our website: http://www.upress.umn.edu. For back issues, contact the Vernacular Architecture Forum. *Buildings & Landscapes* is a benefit of membership in the Vernacular Architecture Forum. Digital subscriptions to *Buildings & Landscapes* are available online through Project MUSE at https://muse.jhu.edu/.

The Vernacular Architecture Forum is the premier organization in the United States studying ordinary buildings and landscapes. Established in 1979–80 to promote the appreciation of and scholarship on vernacular structures, it is an interdisciplinary organization composed of scholars from many fields, including history, architectural history, geography, anthropology, sociology, landscape history, preservation, and material culture studies. Since its founding, the VAF has played a major role in the academic study and preservation of common buildings. The VAF holds an annual meeting, publishes an electronic newsletter and a journal, and maintains a website.

EDITORS

Michael J. Chiarappa
Washington College
and
Margaret M. Grubiak
Villanova University

REVIEW EDITOR

Amanda C. Roth Clark
Whitworth University

ILLUSTRATION EDITOR

Laura Kilcer VanHuss

EDITORIAL BOARD

Anna Vemer Andrzejewski
University of Wisconsin–Madison

Catherine W. Bishir, editorial advisor
Preservation North Carolina

James Michael Buckley
University of Oregon

Gretchen Buggeln
Christ College, Valparaiso University

Jennifer Cousineau
Parks Canada

Cynthia G. Falk
Cooperstown Graduate Program, SUNY Oneonta

Jeffrey E. Klee
MCBW Architects

Matthew Gordon Lasner
Independent scholar

Richard Longstreth
George Washington University

Sarah Lynn Lopez
University of Pennsylvania

Carl Lounsbury
College of William and Mary

William Moore
Boston University

Louis P. Nelson
University of Virginia

Dell Upton
University of California, Los Angeles

Notes

Notes

BUILDINGS & LANDSCAPES

JOURNAL OF THE VERNACULAR ARCHITECTURE FORUM
VOLUME 31 | NUMBER 1 | SPRING 2024

Georgia LaMair and Cynthia G. Falk	An Interview with Elizabeth Collins Cromley	1
Zoya Brumberg-Kraus	A Bridge at Powell and Clay: Designing Chinese American Community in San Francisco's Chinatown YWCA	12
Tessa Evans	Political Landscapes and Rival Cultural Landscapes in Spanish Louisiana: Antoine Sarrasin and *la Cyprière*	31
Jessica Larson	The Black Built Environment of Benevolence in New York's Tenderloin District: Comparative Architectural Approaches to Race, Reform, and Discipline, 1865–1910	54

Reviews

Poplar Forest: Thomas Jefferson's Villa Retreat by Travis C. McDonald
REVIEW BY CLIFTON ELLIS

75

Reconstructing the Landscapes of Slavery: A Visual History of the Plantation in the Nineteenth-Century Atlantic World by Dale W. Tomich, Rafael de Bivar Marquese, Reinaldo Funes Monzote, Carlos Venegas Fornias
REVIEW BY ASIEL SEPÚLVEDA

78

For the Temporary Accommodation of Settlers: Architecture and Immigrant Reception in Canada, 1870–1930 by David Monteyne
REVIEW BY CATHERINE BOLAND ERKKILA

80

Home beyond the House: Transformation of Life, Place, and Tradition in Rural China by Wei Zhao
REVIEW BY JING XIE

82

GEORGIA LAMAIR AND CYNTHIA G. FALK

An Interview with Elizabeth Collins Cromley

As we navigate the first quarter of the twenty-first century, we often measure time pre- and post-pandemic. This interview stems from a pre-pandemic effort by the Vernacular Architecture Forum (VAF) to document its own history through a series of oral histories. In 2018 and 2019, at the last two VAF annual meetings before the COVID-19 shutdown forced conferences in 2020 and 2021 to go virtual, thirteen early members of VAF shared their stories and allowed them to be recorded, transcribed, and archived. This is the second to be published in *Buildings & Landscapes*, the first being Richard Longstreth's, which appeared in the Spring 2019 volume.[1]

Students of vernacular architecture will find Elizabeth Collins Cromley's name a familiar one (Figure 1). Cromley coedited with Carter L. Hudgins *Shaping Communities*, volume six in the *Perspectives in Vernacular Architecture* series, the forerunner to *Buildings & Landscapes*.[2] With Tom Carter, she coauthored *Invitation to Vernacular Architecture: A Guide to the Study of Ordinary Buildings and Landscapes* in 2005.[3] The volume was the first in VAF's special series, which publishes short, well-illustrated volumes that explore central issues in vernacular architecture studies in an accessible and engaging format. *Invitation to Vernacular Architecture* quickly became the go-to introduction to the open-ended, people-based questions and field-based research methodologies that are at the heart of the VAF. Cromley went on to author a second volume in the special series entitled *Experiencing American Houses: Understanding How Domestic Architecture Works* (2022), once again demonstrating her ability to reach a broad readership and provide an initiation to the field of vernacular architecture, this time focusing more explicitly on the most intimate and personal of spaces.[4]

Cromley's oral history begins with her own introduction to the Vernacular Architecture Forum while she was a graduate student in New York City. She received her PhD from the Department of Art History at the City University of New York Graduate School. Her academic career included teaching positions at both the State University of

Figure 1. Elizabeth "Betsy" Collins Cromley. Photograph by C. Lamb.

New York (SUNY) Buffalo and Northeastern University, where she taught architectural history to architecture students preparing to shape the next generation of professionally designed buildings. As Cromley narrates the story of her academic career, her oral history paints a fuller picture of her involvement with a group of like-minded learners who focused on the everyday built environment. To this VAF cohort, she is Betsy, and her work on urban apartments expanded the scope of what constitutes vernacular architecture and what fieldwork looks like.

Betsy Cromley narrated her story with Georgia LaMair, who at the time was a student at the Cooperstown Graduate Program at SUNY Oneonta. LaMair, Karina (Kowalski) Filipowski, Mary Kate Kenney, and Lindsey Marshall traveled to Alexandria, Virginia, under the direction of professor Cindy Falk for the 2018 Vernacular Architecture Forum conference to conduct oral histories. Two more Cooperstown students, Kirbie Sondreal and Jennifer Vos, joined Filipowski in conducting more oral histories with early VAF members in 2019 in Philadelphia, Pennsylvania. The Cooperstown Graduate Program provides a two-year course of study leading to a master's degree in museum studies. Students receive training and experience in conducting oral histories as part of the curriculum under the direction of William Walker. The VAF Oral History Project provided an excellent opportunity to put their oral history skills to work while also being exposed to the study of vernacular architecture, augmenting their material culture coursework with Falk.

The transcript of Cromley's oral history was transcribed by LaMair with minimal editing for clarity. Minor alterations were made to facilitate readability in this print format. Betsy's personality, laughter, and tone only begin to emerge from the words on these pages, but are more fully evidenced in the audio recording, which will become part of the Vernacular Architecture Forum archives housed at Historic New England in Boston, Massachusetts. Special thanks to Carl Lounsbury for the photographs of Cromley taken at VAF annual meetings.

Georgia LaMair (GL): This is Georgia LaMair interviewing Betsy Cromley on May 5, 2018, at the 2018 Vernacular Architecture Forum conference in Alexandria, Virginia, for the Vernacular Architecture Forum's Oral History Project. Betsy, what was your path into VAF?

Betsy Cromley (BC): My path—well it was 1980. I had been finishing my graduate work in New York at the CUNY [City University of New York] grad school, and I had taken several years out to raise my twins, so I was back in school, but I was older than some people. I saw a notice in some newsletter somewhere that said paper proposals were being invited for this vernacular architecture meeting, the first meeting of the Vernacular Architecture Forum. In 1979, they had an organizational meeting with people mostly around the Washington, D.C., area and Virginia and the Chesapeake—people who already knew each other. So, they decided to invite papers and launch the VAF. I had seen this notice, and I sent in a paper proposal, and they accepted it.

They held the meeting at George Washington University. I didn't know anybody because I had been living in New York. I was just about to start my tenure-track job at SUNY Buffalo, so I didn't know any of the Chesapeake people at all, but they invited me to come and give my paper. My paper was on an urban topic, about how people renovate their houses in the boroughs of New York City. I had done the research part of it with two sociologists, who did the oral history part of it. I got access to all the interview material, and I put it together in a paper. So, when I got there the people that I met said, "Wait a second, who are you? Where do you come from? We thought we knew everyone who was doing vernacular architecture." They thought that rural architecture was the only thing in the vernacular category, and it isn't. Urban architecture that is not architect designed is much more of what I wanted to look at. There's much more to how the owners and the residents and the inhabitants have shaped it and changed it. Those are the kinds of questions that we raise when looking at vernacular buildings, and we raise the same questions in the city as we do in the country. Just because it's not a barn doesn't mean it's not vernacular architecture. So that was my introduction to all the people involved in the original VAF. I gave my paper, and I got to meet a whole lot of the people who are still here at this meeting. So that was step one, I'd say.

GL: Who founded VAF?

BC: A bunch of Chesapeake people. I think Catherine Bishir was at that organizational meeting. Dell Upton, Cary Carson, Bob St. George, and John Pierce, who was at George Washington University in American Studies. I'm not sure who else, but Catherine Bishir can tell you a whole list of people who were at the organizational meeting in 1979. Then in 1980 when they invited people to submit paper proposals, the meeting was in a sort of auditorium-type space at George Washington University, and maybe there were a hundred people there—a lot of people.

But the original committee was a smaller group, and they were sort of basing themselves on a group in England, the Vernacular Architecture Group (VAG). Some of the people in the Chesapeake region who'd been interested in vernacular building methods had gone to VAG meetings in England and knew some of those people. When the VAF was founded, they were thinking it was kind of modeled on this English group, except of course, the buildings we work with are much more recent. The VAG people were looking at medieval barns and fourteenth-century chicken coops, and we don't have that. We were looking at the seventeenth century as the earliest stuff and using a variety of methods.

I think that's always been the strength of the VAF. Some people were trained in archaeology or American studies, and my degree is in art history. Others were just straight historians. Some people are architects and builders. There is a big range of specialties. Some people are trained in folklore. So, every time you come to a meeting you hear people talk about buildings from all these different angles, and that's been incredibly valuable in helping every single person open their eyes to alternative ways of looking and the different kinds of information that you can glean from different disciplinary specialties. That's been a really important part of how the whole thing has benefited all of us.

GL: Can you tell me a little bit more about your original study of urban vernacular architecture?

BC: Yes, when I started my graduate work, I was living in Manhattan. I was always interested in architecture, but the departments that were available to get a degree from were art history departments that had architectural history as a component in the art history program. I was always interested in architecture, although I took all kinds of art history courses, too, and I taught art history for eight years before I was able to get a job where I could really specialize in architectural history. But since I was living in Manhattan, when it came time for a dissertation, I was looking at what kind of research materials I had access to, and I had been interested in apartment houses and the architects of apartment houses and what they looked like and so on (Figure 2). There was very little in the way of scholarship on apartment buildings, so I decided I was going to take that on as my dissertation. That ended up being my book *Alone Together*.[5] I lived in apartment buildings, so I knew how they worked, and I had friends who lived in apartment buildings, so I would see them all the time. When the VAF talks about fieldwork I think they pretty much imagine you put your snake-proof pants on and crawl under a porch somewhere with a tape measure. That wasn't exactly my fieldwork, but I knew those kinds of buildings, the apartment houses. I knew how they worked. I saw a range of dates [for their construction] just walking around on the street and visiting friends in apartments, and so I got really involved in figuring out where apartments came from. Why did New Yorkers start building them, why did they start living in them, why didn't they just stay in private houses the way people always say Americans want to do?

In my dissertation I didn't know how to ask good enough questions, so I stuck to the buildings, the physical plan and circulation patterns and ornament and massing and so on. Very much visual stuff about the buildings. But once I started converting that to a book, I figured out

Figure 2. The Dakota, Henry Hardenbergh, 1884, Central Park West and West Seventy-Second Street, New York, New York. From *Sanitary Engineer* 11 (February 1885): preceding page 271.

other kinds of questions I needed to ask, which were much more about class and comparing middle-class and upper middle-class apartment buildings with their sources in Paris for one, and their counterexamples of tenement buildings for the working class, which were already in New York and being used by the poor (Figure 3). I tried to figure out why middle-class people would choose to live this way when they hated the idea of the poor being a model. You didn't want to say, "I'm living in a tenement," you wanted to live in a private house, and people with a fair amount of money couldn't afford the private house because real estate prices were so high then, almost no one had access to a private house. They didn't want to live in a French building either because they thought the French were immoral. So, I tried to just figure out why would people go there [to apartments]. What did they want? How did they find what they wanted in apartment buildings? What did apartments offer to them that they couldn't even have in a private house, such things as telephones and electricity, much earlier than private houses could have? When the dissertation finally became a book, which took me a long time, I answered a lot of those social questions. It turned out to be a real interesting book, I say [laughs], but many people thought it was a very interesting book because it accounted for motivation and why people wanted to go in this direction as well as what architects decided. How did they figure out how to put the building together? It was a lot of the social stuff along with the physical buildings. So that's what that was. I was sticking with an urban theme there because that's where I was living, and I had kids in school, and it wasn't like I could take off and do research in Florence. Life constraints kept me there, and it turned out to be the perfect thing. I had the New York Public Library, which is an incredible resource and had everything I needed except for when I went to Paris for a little while to do some comparative research.

The other project that I mentioned was where I worked with sociologists who talked to something like 120 people who had renovated their houses in Brooklyn and Queens and the Bronx, maybe Hoboken, all peripheral to Manhattan. They interviewed people who had real plain, ordinary houses that they enhanced, you know, in whatever ways they decided to do it. Sometimes it was vinyl siding, and sometimes it was imitation stone that people put on their façades. I've seen it around here in Alexandria [Virginia]. Different window treatments and different door treatments, and so on, different colors. We talked to people about how they imagined what they were doing, why did they choose this over that, and what was their goal in making these improvements to their houses. It was very interesting, and I published an article on that, I forget when, in the early eighties [1982], sticking with an urban theme.[6]

GL: After your first meeting with the VAF, what was your next interaction with them or what did you do with them after?

BC: Okay so that was the first of the annual meetings, which is now thirty-eight or something in that range.

GL: Yes.

BC: Yes, so, I came to the annual meetings—we started having annual meetings—and they were here and there, all around. I got to know from the very first meeting that I connected to all these people because they were asking similar questions to what I wanted to ask. But up to that point the national meeting that you could go to if you were

Figure 3. Reform tenements at the corner of Hicks and Warren Streets, Brooklyn, New York. Elizabeth Bisland, "Cooperative Housekeeping in Tenements," *Cosmopolitan* 8 (November 1889): 35.

interested in architecture was the Society of Architectural Historians [SAH]. And of course, those people were much more attached to professional architects' high-style work, elite clients, expensive buildings, all that. I certainly had gone to SAH meetings, but I didn't find it congenial and as soon as I met the other VAF people I realized, "Oh, this is where I belong," and "Oh, this is what I'm doing, it's vernacular architecture that I'm doing, and it's not violating all the principles of architectural history by going and looking at the working class." It was a great relief to find out that there was kind of a name for what I was doing and a group of people who were sympathetic and that I could hang out with and, at least once a year, go to this meeting and see buildings in a new area.

When they started their annual meetings, every meeting was in a different geographical space. We saw what people were building in the Sanpete Valley in Utah and then what people were building in Wisconsin when they pioneered in the 1850s. Each place, you would see a new vocabulary, new building materials, and you got to have a feel for what's national and what's local, how a region deals with a national style or something like that. Also, the differences that come along with ethnicity or the differences that come along with a particular decade. You started to see these things on the ground for real, not just read about them or *not* read about them because people weren't publishing vernacular architecture in architectural history sources. They weren't looking at these buildings or thinking about what they mean. Each year our knowledge got bigger because we kept going to a new region and looking at a new set of buildings. It added up to a huge amount of learning in those early years and then that learning was compounded by the fact that people came at it from different disciplines. So, that was really very important. Louis Nelson said last night something about this: until he ran into the VAF he didn't sort of know exactly where his career was going, but once he found this institution, he could sort of plug into that, and his career took off, and he was able to define it better and pursue it better. The VAF is the reason why. I'd say many of us feel that way, that our careers took the direction they did because we had each other to bounce ideas off of, and we kept adding to our knowledge every year by coming to these meetings.

The field trips are the big difference between the SAH, where there are papers and papers and papers, and if you were lucky there was a bus trip (not that you would actually learn much from the trip). The VAF has always been attached to field-work, and so you have to go be there and see the building and touch the moldings and, you know, sense the ceiling height, all those things that the physical building tells you. The field trips have always been a major component and then, you know, the papers. In the early years, we would have some papers after dinner, the papers were a little bit less central. Finally, they decided to have the papers all together on one day and two days of field trips, how ever the organizers wanted those to work. The self-guided tours were one way, and the bus tours were another way. I have not myself organized any of the meetings—I know there're plenty of issues that require a huge amount of labor—but the field trips have always been such a learning component of what we do.

GL: Are there any ways that the meetings in the beginning were different from now or have changed since then?

BC: Yes, we are forty years older than we were then [laughs]. It's shocking to us to realize how old we are. We have no idea. How could that be? But, you know, there is a way in which we, the old guard, feel like we grew up together. I was talking to somebody about this on the bus, how other people go to their high school reunion or go to their college reunion, but we come to the VAF in the same exact way, can't wait to see these people. We feel like they've been lifelong companions, and here they are again and isn't it wonderful to see you and that kind of thing. So, there's been an awful lot of bonding with the other people in the group from the beginning, friendships that have lasted thirty-eight years.

So, you said what was different then from now, and I think a really important component of our experience with it is we were just beginning at the beginning. Then we were just kind of forming our careers and now we've had them. I am retired and so are various other people, and so the way we want to learn things is very different now. We don't need to learn to teach anymore because we aren't teaching anymore. When I retired from teaching, I stopped knowing what it was the photograph was for. You know, you go out with your camera and you're taking pictures of this building, and it was always to fit into a lecture in my mind that I wanted to be able to give (Figure 4). When I stopped teaching, all of a sudden I didn't know what my camera was for. Why did I need a picture? Now I've kind of come back around to seeing that its valuable to me to go back over the photos and sort of relive the meeting and think about the issues that were brought up and the papers and things like that, but I no longer have a public purpose for the photographs, so I had to kind of relearn what the camera is for. That's a difference.

We used to stay up really late and drink after the field trips. We'd go back to somebody's room with a bottle of bourbon or something. There was a kind of party feeling, speaking for myself, there were people that I just loved seeing, and it was just great hearing about what they did last year and what their life was like and what they were writing, and you know just getting back together again, and it was so fun. We had much more energy, and we would stay up late and hang out. There used to be a lot of dancing, at the banquet dancing was a big thing. I don't have the energy now. I don't stay up late anymore. I think that kind of party component for me, it certainly faded into the background. Maybe you guys will take that on.

Of course, when you've been publishing articles and books, you know your career has its shape. You know that the area you've dug into or that you've become known for is sort of complete in a way, which is very different from when we started out and didn't know for sure where we were going in terms of our research careers. I think the VAF helped us all to shape where that research career went in different ways. I feel very differently now when I hear a paper. It's not going to form the way I teach bungalows or something. I have already done that. It's over, so it's interesting to go hear what other people's research is up to, but it's not going to affect mine the way it did when we were more starting out.

GL: Could you talk a little bit more about your career?

BC: Sure, so I started teaching with a master's before I finished my PhD, and as I said, I was bringing up twins so when they got to be about eleven I went back to graduate school to finish a PhD. I was teaching with my master's, but I didn't have a tenure-track job. So, when I finished my PhD coursework and was embarking on the dissertation, or I guess maybe it was almost done, I got a job, a tenure-track job, in the architecture school in the State University of New York at Buffalo. All of my tenure-track jobs have been in architecture schools. I worked there for eighteen years and developed the history side of the architecture school, developed the slide collection, and was chair in the department from time to time. I placed myself in a professional school setting, rather than a PhD program, so I didn't have doctoral students. You know what I mean? The next generation that some people have, I don't have. I didn't guide any dissertations ever. It was all architecture students.

Then I moved from there to Northeastern University in Boston, again, in a professional program. When I first went to Northeastern, the department was called Art and Architecture. The art side of it was pretty much mainly graphic design, and later they began to do animation and more digital arts stuff. At a certain point, the architecture program split off from the art department and became its own independent architecture school, which you have to do for the architecture school to get accredited. To get accredited it has to be an independent entity. Then I stopped being chair and went to just being a professor within the architecture program. At that time, I think we had, maybe, three historians, and then we hired another one and then we hired another one, so I think they ended up with five historians who took a variety of approaches to architectural history. We were all teaching professional students who were going to become

Figure 4. Betsy Cromley (right) and Kathleen LaFrank (left), both with cameras, at the 1990 Vernacular Architecture Forum annual meeting in Frankfurt, Kentucky. Photograph by Carl Lounsbury.

architects, and that was great. I learned a lot about design by being around those people.

I was department chair there twice. It turned out that I was the kind of person who made the trains run on time. I was very organized, and everybody appreciates that when you're working in a department and the department chair says, "We're having a meeting, and this is exactly what we are going to talk about, and it is going to start at 1:00 and finish at 2:00." And if anybody has a problem, you solve it right away. It turned out that I was good at that. I didn't intend to be an administrator, but it happened that I had the opportunities and that I was good at doing it. So, that was nice, as another kind of learning.

Along the way I wrote this and that. Tom Carter and I did the *Invitation to Vernacular Architecture* book. I forget what year that came out [2005], but it's gone through a second edition [2008, and a third edition, 2014] for University of Tennessee Press.[7] That was the first one in the VAF series that University of Tennessee Press agreed to sponsor. Right now, I'm doing another one for that series that's called *Experiencing*

American Houses.[8] That's about the kinds of things that people do in houses and allows me to skim over the history of American houses in a short book with a lot of pictures, addressed to beginners. I'm trying to use as illustrations houses from not all of the states in the United States but from many of them to show different regions, different classes, and how people have managed the kind of basic tasks that need to be done in a house, tasks like cooking, sleeping, serving a meal, socializing, storing stuff. Circulation is another topic, like how do you get in and out and around the house, because circulation spaces are very often used for socializing, business, and other things that people do. This allows me to bring all the classes in, all the regions in, the time periods, from 1700 to more or less the present, in a short kind of introduction for people to think about how houses work. I'm finishing that now for the VAF series at the University of Tennessee Press. And that's it, I'm not going to write any more books. I've become a silversmith so that's what I'm doing instead.

GL: You mentioned earlier that when you would come to the meetings, you would hear people present papers, or maybe you would travel and that would influence a lecture or some of your research. Can you think of a specific person or meeting that really influenced you?

BC: I think of it more as a kind of general atmosphere of asking new questions and figuring out what that would mean for me. They wouldn't be the same questions that somebody else was asking but rather a general atmosphere of willingness to open up to alternative ways of seeing things. There were a lot of the members in the early years, and still some, who were very interested in building technology. Things such as the tools that were used to build a log cabin or different kinds of wooden joints that would hold the structure together. Topics like that. A lot of interest in the sort of techniques of fabrication. For me, that wasn't ever at the forefront, but I was really glad to hear about it. I came to understand a side of buildings that I hadn't really paid attention to before. Especially rural buildings where you could sometimes see the techniques. You could look at the structure because some of the wall had fallen off so you could see how the framing worked. You could see the pegs in the joints. A lot of that was very informative to me, while at the same time it wasn't the category of building study that I personally wanted to look into.

At the very first meeting, Catherine Bishir gave a paper on Jacob Holt that became an article that's been put into collected essays here and there.[9] She was talking about ideas in architecture in the mid-nineteenth century, maybe a little earlier, that were printed, like the pattern books that architects were publishing, and the way that information had to balance off against regional habits and traditions in building and the desires of clients who were regionally rooted. The article discusses how those two things kind of played off against each other and how Jacob Holt was able to get those things to dovetail in some way—the national standard styles and the locally preferred traditions of building. She explored the way the building plan worked for regional social practices, so the building served clients' needs. That is something that I've always been interested in, and the fact that somebody else was working on that was very reinforcing. Plus, she was working on North Carolina, which is not material I knew. On the other hand, the kinds of questions about how a community's social needs get along with national standards and stylistic preferences, that kind of question was really important to me.

I'm not sure that I mean this, but the papers that I heard and the people I talked to, the most important thing they did for me was reinforce some thoughts rather than give me a whole new zone to work on. So, the building construction people who were interested in materials and tools, that's not something that I wanted to do. I learned a lot from them, and they helped me to find the boundaries of my work, which were not going to take me there. You could say that's a sort of negative way to look, but knowing what I do not want to do is just as important as what I do want to do, I would say. I appreciated the general idea that buildings get made by people, not by architects. I mean, architects make buildings, but they only make four percent of the buildings. But I valued the idea that you look seriously at what people in some general way have decided that they want to have happen in the built world, either because they took up a hammer and did it themselves or because they expressed their preferences for two-bedroom houses instead of one-bedroom houses. The idea that you look to those people and try to find out what they were thinking and what they wanted was a really important idea. The VAF has always been looking that way at buildings. That includes early buildings that had some anonymous source, or maybe people had done research on the carpenters and who they were and knew their names and who they married and their children. The anonymity of the production of architectural ideas from the general public—whether it's rural farmers or urban apartment dwellers, whatever it is—those ideas bubble up and get used, and they're not coming down from trained architects.

That way of looking at things has been extremely important to me, and I would say many of the members of the VAF have used that kind of point of view to talk about whatever it is they want to talk about. I published an article, I don't remember what year [1984], on Riverside Park in New York City that was a designated landmark.[10]

GL: I am familiar with the park.

BC: Yes, well the designated landmark description says it is a design by Frederick Law Olmsted. He was famous, and he did all kinds of things with landscape in the mid-nineteenth century, and we're celebrating Riverside Park because it's a design of his. The article that I wrote was basically alternative histories of Riverside Park. There's one history that's been produced by the Landmarks Commission (I actually did some research for that report), but the research that I did for that report led me to say that's not the only history of this park. The alternative history points out that the park is now three times as big as it was then. The designated park is only a third of what the park is. Olmsted only worked on it for nine months or something, but people have been in various ways working on it ever since. Generation after generation has put something into the park. Either they build Grant's tomb, or they extended the square footage to go north, or they did something with the railroad—or the parks department planted four hundred trees.

Or whatever it was. By the time I finished my alternative history, it made the Olmsted history look so partial and so negligent of what actually happened there. I just wanted to sort of demonstrate that if you ask vernacular questions about change and the participation of a public whose name is not famous than you get a completely different story than the one that you get if you only stuck to famous men. And I thought this is really interesting, to be able to do that.

So that was just kind of a challenge to the standard architectural history that doesn't want to look at change, it wants to look at intactness. As if the building were a painting that's complete at the time it's delivered and that's it. I think that's been a big contribution of vernacular architecture studies. They look at the way the building is a living entity that goes through lifetimes, and new people come to it and they require it to serve them in different ways than the original owner. They add a wing, then they sell it, and somebody else comes along and turns it into a tavern—the whole cycle of renovation and renewal or expansion or contraction or changes of use and ownership. All that kind of stuff affects a building. If you think of it as a work of art like a painting, a painting doesn't change. It's not supposed to change, and if it does change, oh my god, call a restorer. So, I think that vernacular studies have really shifted the way that you look at a building from "it's a work of art thing that's finished" to "it's a living entity that keeps changing over time and that those changes are what tell us about social life." We want to know about social life because buildings are social objects.

GL: How would you describe VAF culture or traditions at the meetings or just as a whole?

BC: I think it's an evolving story, and every time somebody runs a national meeting different things get introduced. We sort of have a pattern of very important field trips and still important but more focused papers. But that doesn't have to always be the case, you know, we can do it differently, and whoever runs the meeting can decide that they'd like some innovation if they want to. I'd say fieldwork has always been at the root, but there's some, I don't know, discussion I would say of what counts as fieldwork. So, when I say I lived in apartment buildings, and I visited them, and I saw them every day—for some people that's not fieldwork because I wasn't measuring every room, or I wasn't engaging with the construction technique. For some people fieldwork requires getting dirty. For other people I think the level of fieldwork has a lot to do with the subject matter. You know, how much fieldwork do you need to find out about this type of building or this set of buildings? Maybe you need a lot, maybe you don't. But still it is a sort of spine for the way we look at buildings, and everybody encourages first-hand knowledge by getting in the building, getting into it in a physical way, or a getting-dirty way, or at least an experiencing way. It's not stuff you read or its not only stuff you read. It's stuff you do with the building and get in it. So, I'd say that's a real important tradition. I think it's flexible, I think it's an organization that's been flexible over the years and invites new possibilities.

Everybody this year was so excited to see how many graduate students came because there have been times when those of us who have been here for the whole run thought, "What's going to happen when we retire and when we step back? Who is going to take our place, and who is going to keep the organization going?" Because I think we all believe that we've made a tremendous contribution to the way people think about architecture, and we want this to continue, and what if it doesn't, what if we don't get replacements for the old guard? This meeting is just great because there are so many new people, and when they sent out the email with the list of attendees and I looked over it and I said, wait—two-thirds of these people I never heard of before! This is so fabulous! All this new influx of people we hope really enjoy what they're doing here and love the meeting and come back and all that. I would say one of our concerns has been to make sure the VAF keeps going and that it's not just our energy that made it go, but all kinds of new people coming in will make it continue. I think it's important that you young people realize that it's your job [laughs] to take on making the institution continue. That was about tradition, right?

GL: What do you hope for the future of VAF?

BC: Well, I think, what I said before about inventing new questions about architecture and how we look at the built environment. What kinds of questions can we ask and what kinds can we answer? And how can we find out things? The research environment has changed radically since we started. The whole digital array of resources we didn't have at the beginning; now you can find out an incredible amount of information on the Web. I think the questions that people want to ask are going to be different ones in the future, and I don't know what they're going to be. But that's the excitement of it—that people come up with new angles.

Historians in the twentieth century started asking class questions a lot, right? You get a lot of historians in the earlier twentieth century for whom class was the main question. And then lo and behold, in, I don't know, 1970 or something, people discovered gender and all of a sudden, my goodness no one ever asked this gender question before, and ethnic questions, you know, what are those ethnic questions, how will they be asked? And where will that lead us? But gender and class and ethnicity are certainly not the list of all the questions you can ask. There's lots of other kinds of questions, and we don't know what those are yet. Sometimes I wonder how they'll be formulated. It's not that questions all get answered, but they are essential for asking. Right? Because they give you a new angle into whatever it is you're looking at. There's been a bunch of work about space for women, analyzing how houses work for women, and advice given to women about housekeeping, and Catherine Beecher or whatever, but nobody asks anything about men. Hardly ever—I know there is one article on the bachelor flat that I've read. Maybe there's more, but the male bachelor, how is his dwelling, his single-room dwelling, different from other people's? You know there is a whole zone about how masculinity has shaped the built environment that nobody has gotten to yet. So, I guess, that's what I hope for, that the next generation will have interesting questions, and we'll say, "Ah, I never thought of that." That'd be great.

GL: Are there any other topics that we didn't cover about VAF that you can think of, or you want to talk about?

BC: Not so much, I'll just reiterate the importance of friendship (Figure 5). When we got to know each other, we turned to each other when we had, I don't know, a question that we wanted to talk about with somebody. Or a personal thing we wanted to talk about, or the progress of our career, how to get promoted. Or will you write a letter for me so I can get a grant? Or all those things that we got to know about each other at a point when our careers were relatively young, some younger than others. I think that we kind of bounced off of each other as our careers developed in just really crucial ways. We knew we could turn to each other and say, "I think you dealt with this, how do I deal with it?" Or maybe it was an issue in teaching, or we sometimes would share a syllabus. All kinds of things that we helped each other out with. Even in really tiny ways. Just the thought that we had a bunch of friends who were working in a similar direction was so reinforcing and so helpful, it helped you to trust that you were doing the right thing. You weren't wasting your time, and that it was okay to go against the tradition of architectural history or other kinds of history. It was fine to go against those. And we knew that was fine because we had each other's back. That feeling has been really important to me and others in the organization. And may it also be for you.

AUTHOR BIOGRAPHY

Georgia LaMair is the public programs manager at the Zuccaire Gallery at Stony Brook University and a graduate of the Cooperstown Graduate Program. Her work focuses on museum education, exhibitions, and public history.

Cynthia G. Falk coordinated the VAF Oral History Project and is Assistant Dean of Graduate Studies at SUNY Oneonta and professor of material culture at the Cooperstown Graduate Program. She was coeditor of *Buildings & Landscapes* from 2012 to 2017.

NOTES

1. Mary Kate Kenny and Cynthia G. Falk, "An Interview with Richard Longstreth," *Buildings & Landscapes* 26, no. 1 (Spring 2019): 1–10.

Figure 5. Betsy Cromley (second from left) relaxing with Camile Wells (first from left), Claire Dempsey (third from left), and Laura Driemeyer (fourth from left) while listening to a German oompah band at the Daniel Boone Homestead, Birdsboro, Pennsylvania, 2004 Vernacular Architecture Forum Annual Meeting. Photograph by Carl Lounsbury.

2. Carter L. Hudgins and Elizabeth Collins Cromley, eds., *Shaping Communities: Perspectives in Vernacular Architecture, VI* (Knoxville: University of Tennessee Press, 1997).

3. Thomas Carter and Elizabeth Collins Cromley, *Invitation to Vernacular Architecture: A Guide to the Study of Ordinary Buildings and Landscapes,* Vernacular Architecture Studies, ed. Diane Shaw (Knoxville: University of Tennessee Press, 2005, 2008, 2014).

4. Elizabeth Collins Cromley, *Experiencing American Houses: Understanding How Domestic Architecture Works,* Vernacular Architecture Studies, ed. Alison K. Hoagland (Knoxville: University of Tennessee Press, 2022).

5. Elizabeth Collins Cromley, *Alone Together: A History of New York's Early Apartments* (Ithaca, N.Y.: Cornell University Press, 1990, 1998).

6. Elizabeth Collins Cromley, "Modernizing: Or, 'You've Never Seen a Screen Door on Affluent Homes,'" *Journal of American Culture* 5, issue 2 (Summer 1982): 71–79.

7. Carter and Cromley, *Invitation to Vernacular Architecture.*

8. Cromley, *Experiencing American Houses.*

9. Catherine W. Bishir, "Jacob W. Holt: An American Builder," *Winterthur Portfolio* 16, no. 1 (Spring 1981): 1–31, repr. in *Common Places: Readings in American Vernacular Architecture,* ed. Dell Upton and John Michael Vlach (Athens: University of Georgia Press, 1986), 447–81.

10. Elizabeth Cromley, "Riverside Park and Issues of Historic Preservation," *Journal of the Society of Architectural Historians* 43, no. 3 (October 1984): 238–49.

ZOYA BRUMBERG-KRAUS

A Bridge at Powell and Clay

Designing Chinese American Community in
San Francisco's Chinatown YWCA

ABSTRACT

Recently, scholars of Asian American studies and architecture have been revisiting Chinatown architectural design as a unique form. Much of that research focuses on the pagoda-adorned Chinatown architecture of commercial buildings like restaurants, banks, and theaters to appeal to tourists. This article explores the 1932 Young Women's Christian Association (YWCA) Clay Street Center and Residence in San Francisco's Chinatown as an example of vernacular Chinatown architecture that breaks from the standard image of the early twentieth-century Oriental style. I argue that the YWCA's function as a nonprofit community space allowed the women who designed it to portray a creative vision of Chinese American identity that shares some visual continuity with, but is uniquely distinct from, most iconic Chinatown architecture. I also argue that, in a moment when Chinatown was still very much segregated from the rest of San Francisco, the Chinese YWCA board working with architect Julia Morgan used architecture as a medium of pleasure and aspirational visual integration for working-class immigrant women.

As I walked through San Francisco's Chinatown the summer of 2021, the losses of the last year due to COVID-19 were palpable. The strings of paper lanterns, wrought iron trellises decorated with Chinese characters, and antique neon Chop Suey signs glowed across Chinatown, but the streets were emptier than I remembered (Figure 1). Grant Avenue, Chinatown's central commercial street, was blocked off from cars to accommodate pedestrians and outdoor diners. Most of the neighborhood's historic bars and theaters were boarded up. A landscape transformed by COVID-19 was a strong reminder of Chinatown's historical precarity, a place where the ghosts of America's Chinese Exclusion Act and segregation still cast a long shadow on what is primarily a tourist destination in the twenty-first century. Though the museum of the Chinese Historical Society of America, which is now housed in the

former 1932 Chinatown Young Women's Christian Association (YWCA) complex by architect Julia Morgan, was closed, a banner for the exhibition Chinese American Exclusion/Inclusion was draped above the window. The sign still reads "YWCA" in both Chinese characters and Roman letters, despite the new function as a museum (Figure 2).

The words written concretely on the surfaces of San Francisco's Chinatown YWCA reflect deeper histories inscribed in the neighborhood's architecture. The early twentieth-century buildings in San Francisco stand as an archive of one of America's racially segregated neighborhoods and the largest concentration of Chinese immigrants on the West Coast.[1] In the decade following the earthquake of 1906, a Chinatown-Beautiful movement was initiated, spearheaded by Chinese American businessmen including community leaders Look Tin Eli and Lew Hing. San Francisco's Chinatown was the first urban center to undergo a neighborhood-wide architectural transformation. The buildings that sought to erase negative images of Chinatown as an urban ghetto and rebrand it as a tourist destination ushered in the familiar pagoda-adorned Chinatown architecture and other variations of Chinatown style across the United States. Because of this history, Chinatown architecture is often contextualized as a marketing tool, explored through its use in restaurants and other commercial buildings. The Chinatown YWCA—a complex consisting of a community center fronting Clay Street and a segregated residence for Chinese and White women spanning Clay and Powell Streets—incorporates some of these visual characteristics, but it was designed for and by a community of Chinese American women rather than to serve the touristic gaze.

This article presents a counternarrative to the commercial theory of Chinatown architecture through the example of the Chinatown YWCA Clay Street Center and Residence at the intersection of Powell and Clay Streets, which combined Tuscan-inspired structures with elements of the so-called Oriental style for their own community's consumption without the motivation of commercial profit (Figure 3). The Chinese American board of directors collaborated with architect Julia Morgan to design a building that could express pride in the board's own cultural heritage while embracing American freedoms and modernity.[2] They designed the building to suit the needs of working-class Chinese American women who wanted to learn English, pursue higher education, work for wages, live independently, and exercise for physical health. White-led charity organizations like the Donaldina Cameron House, also in San Francisco's Chinatown, offered some of these opportunities, but racialized hierarchies were ingrained in these institutions, which promoted a program of Anglo-Protestant Americanization. In contrast, the Chinese American women who led the local YWCA chapter incorporated Chinese cultural education and services into the national program at the request of the women served by the organization. The hybrid style of this community space presented a new image of modern Chinese American women in San Francisco.

Both the visual and functional aspects of the Chinatown YWCA building and its residence signified the compromises that Chinese American women had to make to live in San Francisco. At the request of the Chinese American women on the Chinatown YWCA's board of directors, Julia Morgan combined her characteristic redbrick Renaissance revival style with contemporary Chinese design elements so that the space would reflect both its ideological and practical functions. While markedly different from the surrounding

Figure 1. View of Grant Avenue in San Francisco's Chinatown, June 2021. Photograph by Zoya Brumberg-Kraus.

Figure 2. Detail of the sign on San Francisco's Chinatown YWCA, featuring both Chinese characters and Roman letters, photographed June 2021. Photograph by Zoya Brumberg-Kraus.

commercial pagoda architecture, the building visually connected with its location in San Francisco's Chinatown. Notably, the YWCA's Clay Street Center was connected to the Residence that served both the Anglo-dominant Nob Hill neighborhood and Chinese women. Though it was physically connected to the Chinatown YWCA, the Residence was racially segregated. The Chinese American women who directed the YWCA, as well as those who utilized its services, had to navigate their identities both as Chinese Americans within prejudiced White women's organizations and as women within patriarchal Chinese society. Distinct from Chinatown-Beautiful movement leader Look Tin Eli's "Oriental palaces," which presented Chinese-influenced façades for an emerging tourist economy, the Chinatown YWCA incorporated Chinese decorative elements within the functional structure of the building

Figure 3. Street view of the Chinatown YWCA's Clay Street Center (1932) by architect Julia Morgan. Photograph by Kristen Sheets.

for the aesthetic pleasure of the women who used the YWCA and resided in the Residence. At the corner of Powell and Clay Streets, these buildings bridged their Chinese heritage and modern American womanhood both through the design of the building and its geographic position between Nob Hill and Chinatown.

Chinatown-Beautiful

The iconic Chinatown architecture that is so ubiquitous today—dubbed the Oriental style by its early proponents such as Look Tin Eli—was largely inspired by the necessity to rebuild the Chinatown neighborhood following San Francisco's massive 1906 earthquake.[3] The earthquake devastated much of the Bay Area, but its effect on Chinatown was compounded by years of systemic neglect and a preexisting political impetus to obliterate the neighborhood. The earthquake ruptured gas lines, causing uncontrollable fires to spread across the city. The quake also cut off water mains, and assistant fire chief John H. Dougherty decided that the only way to stop the fire was to dynamite buildings before it consumed them. His tactic instead accelerated the fires, burning down the majority of San Francisco's Chinatown.

Even though the neighborhood was made uninhabitable by the quake, fires, and dynamite, Chinese San Franciscans were barred from renting property or operating businesses elsewhere in the city. There was some talk of relocating the district to Hunter's Point, but no other neighborhoods wanted to be associated with Chinatown.[4] Relocating Chinese Americans elsewhere would have required the city of San Francisco to amend its restrictive zoning laws, potentially giving middle-class and wealthy Asian Americans access to housing in White neighborhoods. Furthermore, White absentee landlords could overcharge Chinese renters because they were barred from renting elsewhere or owning property.[5] Chinese Americans who relied on living and working in the area had to find a way to rebuild Chinatown. The need was immediate, yet restoring Chinatown was not a priority for a municipal government that had abandoned it well before it was physically destroyed.

San Francisco's city government designated Chinatown a slum and refused to provide necessary services like sanitation and hospitals to the area. Chinese American elites and philanthropists intervened in a moment of critical need. Most Chinese Americans—even wealthy ones—were unable to operate their businesses outside of Chinatown. It was in Chinese American elites' economic interests to revive and support Chinatown, even if they had the connections to circumvent San Francisco's anti-Chinese zoning.[6] Wealthy Chinese business owners like banker Look Tin Eli, cannery owner Lew Hing, and newspaper producer Ng Poon Chew were not able to purchase property outright due to California's alien land laws. Instead, they signed long-term leases for tracts of land on which they could build structures in the Oriental style. Many of these wealthy Chinese elites used their connections to live outside of Chinatown, but those whose businesses catered to Chinese clientele relied on Chinatown as a site of commerce.[7] For those with means, the devastated neighborhood presented an opportunity to design a new Chinatown that could rebrand San Franciscans' perceptions of their Chinese neighbors.[8]

Look Tin Eli—a merchant, banker, and secretary of the Chinese Chamber of Commerce—was the public face for the aesthetic and social transformation of San Francisco's Chinatown. He imagined an "Oriental City" in the mode of architect Daniel Burnham's City Beautiful, a design movement that promoted social reform through meticulously planned urban environments that were clean, spacious, and attractive.[9] In direct reference to the movement, Eli named his version Chinatown-Beautiful in the 1910 Western Press Association guidebook *San Francisco: The Metropolis of the West,* in a section titled, "Our New Oriental City—Veritable Fairy Palaces Filled with the Choicest Treasures of the Orient."[10] Eli's investors—including his father Look Eli and Pacific Coast Canning Company owner Lew Hing—provided the majority of the financial support for the Sing Chong and Sing Fat Bazaars and spearheaded Chinatown's revival outside the public eye.[11] Hing was an older, first-generation Chinese immigrant and the most influential

Chinese American businessman in the Bay Area at the time.[12] When the earthquake totaled the Pacific Coast Canning factory in Oakland, Hing erected tents on the factory site to offer food and shelter to numerous Chinese refugees of the 1906 earthquake.[13] Because many members of the Bay Area's Chinese American community relied on Hing as their employer and benefactor, he worked to avoid any anti-Chinese backlash he might face as a public figure transforming San Francisco's Chinatown. To avoid this backlash, Eli and Hing created a mutually beneficial relationship: Eli would be the public face and voice of Chinatown-Beautiful, and Hing would provide the funds to realize it.

While Eli envisioned structures that would evoke White tourists' ideas of what Chinese buildings should look like, he also stressed the need for the structures to be functional and modern. Eli thought that hiring White male commercial architects based in San Francisco—and inspired by the beaux arts tradition—would make his designs more approachable and respectable to non-Chinese patrons.[14] With Lew Hing's financial backing, Eli commissioned the non–Chinese American commercial architecture firm Ross & Burgren (composed of architect T. Paterson Ross and engineer A. W. Burgren) to design pagoda-style buildings for his Sing Chong and Sing Fat Bazaars. Ross had designed the chapel at Cypress Lawn Cemetery (1892) south of San Francisco and a number of residential homes prior to 1906, but Ross & Burgren developed their reputation as key figures in the post-earthquake reconstruction of the city.[15] Their best-known buildings between 1906 and 1908 were the seven-story fireproof Clunie Office Building, Hotel Jefferson, Baldwin Apartments, and Hotel Avalon.[16] Both Ross and Burgren likely got their architectural training through night classes in San Francisco and by working as draftsmen for more established local architects John Gash and Charles J. Colley, respectively.[17] The women of the Chinatown YWCA would later work with a woman architect, Julia Morgan, who was actually formally trained at the École des Beaux-Arts in Paris. Along with Morgan, Ross & Burgren were known for their talents at accommodating their designs to work with the California environment, where steep topography and frequent earthquakes presented engineering challenges.[18]

Architectural historian Philip Choy wrote that Ross & Burgren's "challenge [in Chinatown] was to transform these ancient forms into a new Sino-architectural vocabulary using Western methods of construction and local building materials in conformance with local building codes."[19] The Sing Chong and neighboring Sing Fat Bazaars were housed in steel-framed commercial brick buildings, topped with multilevel steel-frame pagodas (Figures 4 and 5). In China, the multitiered pagoda housed religious objects and denoted a site as a place of worship, but in these commercial properties in San Francisco's Chinatown, pagodas were secular and purely ornamental. Both buildings were illuminated at night by several thousand incandescent light bulbs. The Trigram logo (a Taoist symbol) on Sing Chong and the dragon trademark of Sing Fat embodied the exotic Oriental image that would attract non-Chinese clientele to Look Tin Eli's businesses.

Eli's Chinatown-Beautiful benefited San Francisco's tourism economy on a citywide scale. Politicians lauded the speed and success with which the district was able to bounce back from the earthquake.[20] The San Francisco Real Estate Board endorsed Eli's "Oriental City," attesting that "the Chinese style of architecture will make [Chinatown] picturesque . . . and attractive to tourists." The board recommended that all property owners in the district "have their buildings re-built with fronts of Oriental and artistic appearance."[21] Eli's Chinatown evoked a sanitized, quaint image of Chinese San Francisco endorsed by White politicians and city planners, distinctly separate from the rest of the city yet integral to its culture and economy. Eli deliberately promoted the neighborhood as a tourist destination to ease relationships between Chinese and non-Chinese Californians.[22]

Look Tin Eli and other Chinese businessmen wanted an architecture to express a neighborhood defined by cultural difference as opposed to poverty and exclusion. Historian Ellen Wu writes:

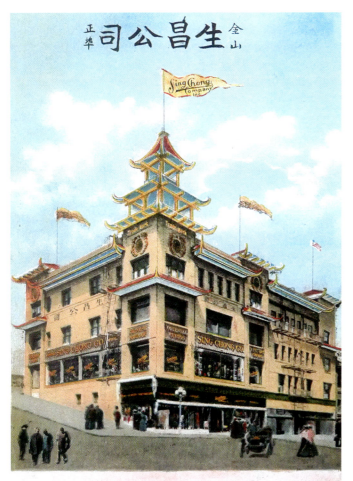

Figure 4. Postcard of the Sing Chong Company Bazaar in San Francisco's Chinatown, circa 1908. From the personal collection of Zoya Brumberg-Kraus.

Figure 5. Postcard of the Sing Fat Company Bazaar in San Francisco's Chinatown, circa 1908. From the personal collection of Zoya Brumberg-Kraus.

Recognizing the enormous retail potential of Chinatown's peculiar sights, sounds, and smells—yet fearful of perpetuating associations between Chinese and iniquity—San Francisco's immigrant planners rallied to promote their neighborhood as a strange yet innocuous place of leisure at the turn of the century.[23]

Their new Chinatown offered restaurants, temples, shops, galleries, and theaters for tourists to enjoy, a marked departure from the "slumming" attractions—prostitutes, opium dens, and gambling—that drew White tourists to the district prior to the earthquake.[24] These aesthetic transformations corresponded with contemporary social reforms.[25] Previous attempts to "clean up" Chinatown were inextricably tied to anti-Chinese biases that blamed the unsanitary and dangerous conditions in Chinatown on the people forced to live there. In this newest iteration, with an old Chinatown cleansed by a natural and manmade disaster, Chinese American community leaders worked with San Francisco's municipal officials to quell the violent conflicts between Chinese gangs known as the Tong Wars, eliminate prostitution, and modernize infrastructure. These changes sanitized the neighborhood of its reputation as a place of vice, and its Chinatown-Beautiful architecture signified the implementation of such changes.

Eli carefully framed the exotic appeal of Chinatown as something that could only exist in the United States. He wrote that Chinatown's "fantastic, Oriental architecture and color scheme cannot be duplicated in the wide world, not even in the Orient, for the reason that in that interesting country the contrasts are entirely too pronounced, and a magnificent palace is frequently surrounded by dozens of ordinary shacks and mat sheds."[26] In this quotation, Eli refers to China and "the Orient" interchangeably, emphasizing their cultural and physical distance from San Francisco's Chinatown. In China, elegant palatial designs were exclusively for the elite yet surrounded by the poverty of a world that had not yet modernized in the Western mode. Poverty was prolific throughout San Francisco Chinatown as well, but Eli presented an aspirational vision of a redesigned Chinatown as a space where ordinary people could experience luxurious design inspired by Chinese wealth in commercial, secular environs. Many of the Chinese-inspired decorative elements and modern amenities in Chinatown would have been inaccessible to most Chinese nationals in China prior to the turn of the century. Eli's architectural intervention promoted American capitalism as an avenue for success, evidenced by the fact that some Chinese Americans—like Lew Hing—were able to achieve more wealth and stability in the United States than their parents could in China, even with the barriers of anti-Chinese violence, discrimination, and exclusion.[27]

Chinatown's remodel relied on façades and surface ornamentation to signify a new, safe Chinatown. Eli and his contemporaries could not design away the poverty and segregation that had defined Chinatown since the nineteenth century. The aesthetic transformation of San Francisco's Chinatown benefited many who lived there but at the price of being Orientalized and stereotyped. This new narrative insisted that "Chinatown's authenticity lay in the exoticism of its architecture, theatrical performances, curios, and cuisine," but as historian Raymond Rast contends, "these claims affirmed perceptions of Chinese Americans as authentic 'others' more systematically and thus more forcefully."[28] Non-elite Chinatown citizens and business owners participated in Chinatown's new image whether or not they embraced the superficial interpretation of Chinese architecture. Most Chinatown residents still lived in poverty, whereas many of the Chinese American elites, including Ng Poon Chew and Lew Hing, were able to buy homes in more spacious, non-Chinese neighborhoods in Oakland.[29] Look Tin Eli lived in the neighboring, mostly White Nob Hill neighborhood.[30] The 1882 Chinese Exclusion Act, alien land laws, high taxes, zoning restrictions, and discrimination in education and occupations stunted true growth and upward mobility for most Chinese Americans. The post-earthquake model was designed to attract tourists, but putting a pagoda on a crowded tenement-style building had little benefit for the day-to-day lives of those who lived there.

The performative style of Chinatown architecture reflected the reality that both elite and working-class Chinese Americans in San Francisco constantly faced the conflicting pressures of assimilation and Orientalization. "Acting Chinese"—wearing traditional costumes for special events; holding lavish festivals; decorating their businesses in stereotypical Chinese accents; sticking to their prescribed occupations in restaurants, import/export retail, laundry, and herbal medicine—gave Chinese Americans control over the connotations of what "Chinese" meant to non–Chinese Americans.[31] For example, the San Francisco Chinese community put on a Miss Chinatown American-style beauty pageant in 1915 as part of the Panama-Pacific International Exposition, where Rose Lew—Chinatown financier Lew Hing's daughter—was crowned Chinatown queen. Lew and the other women who participated in the pageant wore both Western and Chinese-inspired fashion such as qipao dresses.[32] Cultural difference was profitable for Chinese Americans; it enticed Americans who wanted a taste of something exotic but could not afford to leave the country. Yet this market niche reinforced the negative stereotype that Chinese were fundamentally different from White Americans and unassimilable. Chinatowns for tourists replaced negative images of Chinese as dangerous and unsanitary with more innocuous cultural stereotypes. In doing so, these Chinatown performances of "safe" Orientalist stereotypes implied that Chinese culture—and thus Chinese people—were backward or primitive.[33]

Chinese American Women's Vision for the Chinatown YWCA

While Eli's Chinatown-Beautiful movement presented this tourist version of Chinese identity, the Chinese American women on the board of the Chinatown YWCA crafted an alternative vision for its building that catered not to tourists but to Chinese American women themselves (Figure 6). Founded in 1916, the Chinatown chapter of the YWCA became a vital institution for Chinese women in the area by the 1920s, providing educational and social opportunities for Chinese American women who were excluded from White women's spaces and Chinese men's spaces. Six hundred Chinese American women were dues-paying members of the Chinatown YWCA in 1928, and the branch served over fifteen thousand members within the community.[34] Rather than following the programming of the White-led national organization, Chinese women were in charge of policies and programming at the Chinatown YWCA. All but one of the women on the board of directors were Chinese by 1929, and board member Rose (Dongmei) Chew, a social worker and daughter of Chinatown YWCA cofounder Chun Fah Chew, became the first Chinese American director in 1932.[35] Architect Julia Morgan's Chinatown YWCA Clay Street Center and Residence ultimately reflected their recommendations for how to best serve the San Francisco Chinese and Chinese American community. While the Chinatown YWCA used some similar design approaches to Eli's commercial Oriental style, its use of Chinese decorative elements complemented the function of the complex instead of presenting it as an advertisement for the Chinatown Chamber of Commerce. The Chinatown YWCA was designed for the pleasure of the women who inhabited it and not the touristic gaze.

As a Chinese American–led organization, the Chinatown YWCA offered a different model than other nearby charitable women's homes directed by wealthy White Christian women, such as the Methodist Mission led by Katherine Mauer and the Presbyterian Mission Home led by Donaldina Cameron.[36] Although anti-Chinese sentiment exaggerated the prevalence of human trafficking in Chinatown, it was a problem, and these mission organizations sought to serve the many Chinese girls and women who were imported, bought, sold, and traded as prostitutes or indentured servants in the United States.[37] The women rescued from sex trafficking and human slavery in Chinatown would have had complex relationships with the homes that, as Karen McNeill describes it, "schooled them in English, Victorian morality, Christianity, and job skills; offered marriage counseling; and intervened in immigration issues."[38] These organizations provided invaluable services and opportunities to women in Chinatown that were otherwise inaccessible to them in Chinese patriarchal society, but those services were integrally tied to assimilationist ideologies and colonial narratives that reinforced the White nativist idea that there was something inherently pathological in Chinese culture.[39] Of the many Chinese American women who were housed and educated in these institutions, those who found financial stability in adulthood—typically through marrying ministers or merchants—were empowered

Figure 6. Photograph of the Chinatown YWCA board of directors, 1920. Image courtesy of the Chinese Historical Society of America.

by their Christian affiliations to build social connections, push the boundaries of their prescribed gender roles, and conduct charity work in their communities in Chinese-led organizations like the Chinatown YWCA.[40] McNeill argues that the Chinatown YWCA women did not "passively submit to the authority of the White women who ran institutions such as the rescue missions or the [national] YWCA" but instead took control of such organizations to serve their community without abandoning their cultural heritage.[41]

The group of Chinese women who founded the Chinatown YWCA adopted the structures of White Christian women's organizations to become agents of social change in their own community. The programming of the Chinatown YWCA incorporated Chinese cultural activities and education into a Western-style Christian organization. As a neighborhood institution, the Chinatown YWCA also created employment opportunities for the same women who benefited from the programs, in large part because college-educated Chinese American women were denied employment in majority White institutions.[42] The Chinatown YWCA offered English language classes and interpretation services that helped Chinese American women with labor and legal issues. The YWCA also assisted with immigration paperwork, job training, hygiene, childcare, and well-baby programs.[43] Educated bilingual Chinese American women like board member and director Rose Chew, associate secretary Florence Chinn Kwann, and director of programs Jane Kwong Lee applied their translation skills beyond the cultural and linguistic divides between Chinese and White Americans. They took on roles as interpreters to facilitate communication between first and second generations of Chinese American immigrant women.[44] The YWCA conducted programs bilingually and hosted numerous cultural heritage events that felt modern and accessible to younger generations of Chinese American women.[45]

In 1926, it became apparent that the Chinatown YWCA was outgrowing its facilities and needed more room for recreation, education, and housing. The Bay Area regional YWCA approved not only larger quarters but an entire new build-ing project in 1928.[46] Although the majority of the women who founded the Chinatown YWCA were elite representatives of San Francisco's Chinese community, the building was supported through community fundraising that bridged socioeconomic class and multiple generations of Chinese American women.[47] Led by Chinatown YWCA cofounder and community activist Emily Lee Fong, the Chinatown YWCA raised over $10,000 through donations and fundraising when it became apparent that the initial budget of $310,000 would not cover the gymnasium and club rooms.[48] From its very inception, the women on the Chinatown YWCA board were instrumental in designing a complex of buildings that would suit the specific needs of the Chinatown branch of the YWCA.

Collaborative Design: Julia Morgan and the Chinatown YWCA

The first- and second-generation Chinese American women who comprised the Chinatown YWCA board in the 1920s designed the YWCA complex alongside their chosen architect, Julia Morgan. They dictated the resources and spaces that would be most useful to the community. Board member Rose Chew represented the Chinatown YWCA to the regional YWCA building commission, applying her skills as a social worker and interpreter to liaise between the Chinese board and the larger regional organization. From a 1930 survey describing the specific social work needs of San Francisco's Chinese community, Chew identified that one of the major challenges was "helping the younger group, while acquiring western ideals and culture, not to throw away their Chinese heritage, but to appreciate the culture of their parents and to cultivate this appreciation in order to make their lives as American citizens richer by this heritage."[49] The collaboration between the Chinese American board of directors and architect Julia Morgan produced a new Chinatown YWCA complex that reflected the changing status of Chinese women in San Francisco's Chinatown: simultaneously American and Chinese, modern but influenced and inspired by tradition. Morgan and the women on the board of the Chinatown YWCA aimed to design a serious and thoughtful interpretation of contemporary Chinese architecture that embodied the depth of the women who commissioned it, and they worked together to design a complex that suited the needs and desires of the local chapter.

Crucially, Julia Morgan had already designed buildings for women's charities in San Francisco's Chinatown. These organizations were run by White women, but they demonstrate some of the design strategies she would employ for the Chinatown YWCA. In 1908, Morgan designed the Donaldina Cameron House, a school and home for Chinese immigrant women, to replace the Occidental Presbyterian Mission House—the orphanage where Chun Fah Chew, the cofounder of the Chinatown YWCA, was raised before the earthquake.[50] Cameron House was not built in an Asian-influenced style, but Morgan's design was symbolically akin to others that she would later design for Chinese women in Chinatown (Figure 7). She used salvaged bricks from the original building—a material metaphor for resilience. It was also a prudent choice to keep the materials budget low so that the location could be constructed as immediately as possible. The design drew attention to local history by utilizing materials from the original location, and though it referenced an older generation, it was transformed for the modern one.

Shortly thereafter, Morgan designed the Gum Moon Residence (previously named the Methodist Chinese Mission School) in 1909, another Christian home for rescued Chinese women. Gum Moon was fashioned in the beaux arts style, adorned with subtle Asian influences (Figure 8). It was built with red bricks, a popular post-earthquake material because it was seen as being fire resistant. Morgan added jade and gold accents to her signature red brick to evoke traditional color motifs. The Gum Moon Residence looks much the same today, with the addition of Chinese language plaques on both sides of the front door. The tiles that Morgan used to adorn the arch of the 1909 building feature a similar geometric pattern to the imported tiles used in the Chinatown YWCA garden, though the Gum Moon accents appear to be cast from molds made at her atelier.[51] The vaulted doorway

is adorned with a cast stone peony—a flower native to China symbolizing prosperity and luck. The decorative iron balconies connect to fire escapes, having both aesthetic and functional uses. The bright colors currently featured were restored in the 1980s based on recollections of the women who were raised in the mission home.[52] The lantern that hangs over the vaulted doorway also evokes Chinese decorative arts and was possibly purchased from a local Chinese lamp maker, Num Sing, from whom Morgan sourced lamps for other projects (Figure 9).[53] In interviews about his time working for Julia Morgan in the 1920s and 1930s, architect and engineer Walter Steilberg described Morgan's interest in Chinese art and architecture as something she explored and drew from throughout her career,

Figure 7. Photograph of the 1908 Donaldina Cameron House in San Francisco's Chinatown. Architect Julia Morgan used bricks from the previous building destroyed in the 1906 earthquake to construct this replacement. The clinker bricks are arranged with texture that draws attention to the materials used. Photograph by Kristen Sheets.

Figure 8. Street view of the 1909 Gum Moon Residence (previously named the Methodist Chinese Mission School) by architect Julia Morgan in San Francisco's Chinatown. Photograph by Zoya Brumberg-Kraus.

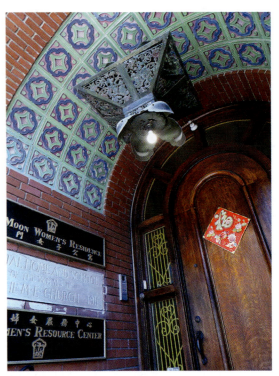

Figure 9. Detail of lantern at the Gum Moon Residence. Photograph by Zoya Brumberg-Kraus.

and it was likely that she developed that interest while designing her early Chinatown buildings.[54]

In designing buildings for the Chinatown YWCA and also for the Japanese YWCA in San Francisco's neighboring Japantown, Julia Morgan took into careful account the perspectives of her Chinese and Japanese women clients. She took the risk of working directly with representatives from the San Francisco Chinatown and Japantown YWCA boards to render designs based on their needs, knowing that the individual chapters would likely need more assistance than the national organization was willing to fund—priorities that local chapters would, in all likelihood, not be able to financially afford. Like the Chinatown YWCA, the building that Morgan designed in 1932 in collaboration with the Japanese American women comprising San Francisco's Japantown YWCA board incorporated elements of Japanese architecture in its design (Figure 10). Morgan was likely sympathetic to the experiences of the Chinese and Japanese American women she built for because she herself faced significant barriers pursuing the male-dominated architecture profession. The vitriol she was subjected to as the first female student at the École des Beaux-Arts in Paris and mistreatment by colleagues earlier in her career instilled her with what Karen McNeill describes as "a strong sense of society's prescribed roles for women and the resulting constraints on her personal and professional development."[55] Male students at the École des Beaux-Arts protested her attendance, and no atelier accepted her until the school established one for women in 1898.[56] Morgan personally understood the difficulties of pursuing a career beyond that which was expected of her, and she was also aware of the risks of being in the limelight.

Though Morgan and many of her friends were of an elite class and educational background, she was known in her circles not only for working with but having close relationships to women across class, racial, and religious lines. For example, Morgan hired Dorothy Wormser, the first Jewish woman architect licensed in California, to work for her atelier and act as the managing architect for the Emanu-El Sisterhood Residence Club.[57] She also had a long-term friendly relationship with her Japanese American housekeeper and friend Sachi Oka, who worked at her home in Monterey, California.[58] Morgan sent letters and supplies to the Oka family during their incarceration during World War II and bought them a home in Monterey so that they could return there after the war, even though their neighbors filed a petition against their return.[59] In her 2022 biography of Morgan, Victoria Kastner frames Morgan's relationship with Sachi Oka as part of Morgan's generous personality, representative of the way that she interacted with many of her friends. Morgan might have seen her experience of being excluded reflected in the experience of the women who worked with Morgan to design the Chinatown and Japantown YWCAs: educated, capable, and ambitious women who, through no fault of their own, were excluded from the lives they wished to pursue.

Working together, the Chinatown YWCA board and Julia Morgan produced a complex of buildings that blended American and European architectural elements with both modern and traditional Chinese design and symbolism. In contrast to the Chinatown-Beautiful style promoted by developer Look Tin Eli and financier Lew Hing from roughly 1907 to 1920, which relied on nonfunctional ornament to express Chinese identity and maximize the contrast to White neighborhoods like Nob Hill, the YWCA's 1932 design fully integrated Chinese decorative elements into a modern Renaissance revival brick building that demonstrated visual continuity between Chinatown and Nob Hill (see Figure 3). This combination of Italian Renaissance revival and Chinatown architecture emphasized the modernity of the Chinatown YWCA women and their identification with Christianity, philanthropy, education, and bourgeois gender roles.[60]

To satisfy the prevailing local prejudice against the Chinese, the original plan for a racially integrated residence was replaced with a racially divided one. The Chinese women's section was attached to the YWCA's Clay Street Center. The Chinese and White women's sections connected to each other externally in the back, joined by a tower echoing the design of the Clay Street Center's pagoda-inspired towers (Figure 11). They were only connected externally; one could not move between the sections from their interiors, and this division is apparent when facing the Powell Street frontage. The back of the White women's section looked over the Clay Street Center's courtyard, and all sides of the building provided sweeping views of Chinatown (Figure 12). Both sections demonstrated through their physical connection and visual continuity that Chinatown was part of San Francisco and not so different from the surrounding city.

Morgan and the women on the board of the Chinatown YWCA aimed to design a serious and thoughtful interpretation of contemporary Chinese architecture that embodied the depth of the women who commissioned it. Within the frame of a Renaissance revival brick building, Morgan and the Chinese American board crafted clearly discernable Chinese elements and a distinctive Chinese American program. The Powell Street entrance to the Residence was designed with a fairly conservative Tuscan revival design (Figure 13). Its roof used the green clay tile of the rest of the building, and the walls facing the shared courtyard were all adorned with Chinese-inspired design elements. The gold, green, and red motif throughout the building evokes traditional Chinese design. The ground-floor Chinese wing opens to a courtyard with a Chinese "cloud lift" detail on its larger windows (Figure 14). A mural of a dragon painted on the floor of the hallway adjacent to the courtyard evokes traditional Chinese elements through a contemporary, playful style (Figure 15). The crenellation surrounding the exterior of the gymnasium—a decorative

Figure 10. The Japantown YWCA, designed by architect Julia Morgan in 1932, at 1830 Sutter Street in San Francisco's Japantown, now the Nihonmachi Little Friends multicultural daycare center. Photograph by Kristen Sheets.

Figure 11. View from Clay Street showing the Chinatown YWCA's Clay Street Center (bottom left), Chinese women's section of the Residence (right), and the rear of the White women's section of the Residence (left). The two sections of the Residence are connected by a tower that combines the shape of the Clay Street Center tower with the color scheme of the Powell Street frontage. The back of the White women's section of the Residence overlooked the Clay Street Center courtyard, whereas the front faced Powell Street. Photograph by Zoya Brumberg-Kraus.

Figure 12. Rear view of the White women's section of the Residence of the Chinatown YWCA. Photograph by Kristen Sheets.

element that evokes European castles—is constructed from specialty tiles imported from China.[61] The large gymnasium—the most overtly American attribute of the building that tied Asian American women to the physical culture movement—was inspired by Chinese rigid frame buildings (Figure 16). Sarah Holmes Boutelle emphasized the uniquely Chinese American significance of the feature, noting that "physical exercise for girls had not been acceptable to most earlier generations" of Chinese women.[62]

These interior decorative and programmatic features, blending Chinese and American identities consciously for the pleasure of the women who used the building, distinguished the Chinatown YWCA from the performative and touristic aspects of the Chinatown-Beautiful buildings that surrounded it even as they shared a common architectural language.[63] The complex's location away from central Chinatown areas like Grant Avenue reinforced that this was a community space and service, not an attraction or commercial building. The Chinese architectural elements of the YWCA complex were not a performance of the exotic, nor were they designed to attract and satisfy tourists, like Eli's "veritable fairy palaces." The value of the Chinatown YWCA was not reliant on White patrons. Rather, the buildings and their decorations were for the pleasure and pride of the Chinese American women who would live in the Residence and utilize the services of the institution. The Chinatown YWCA was an expression of the changing pluralistic landscape of San Francisco's multicultural ethnic makeup as envisioned by the Chinese American women who lived and worked there.

Located at the corner of Powell and Clay Streets, the Chinatown YWCA was intended to be a physical and metaphorical bridge of the racial, class, and economic lines that existed at the border between Chinatown and the wealthy White Nob Hill neighborhood. Leaders of the national YWCA organization had supported the selection of the site because it had the potential to further the national organization's liberal aims toward racial integration. They thought that Julia Morgan's Italian Renaissance revival style, coupled with attractive modern amenities, would be exciting and attractive enough to both Chinese and White women to bring the YWCA's Residence to near full capacity. The San Francisco regional YWCA needed more residential space for its young female members, and housing White and Chinese women in the same structure—built in conjunction with the Clay Street Center community building—was much more cost effective than creating two separate buildings for the adjoining neighborhoods. The location was a risk, however, as the negative stereotypes of Chinatown could make even working-class White women hesitant to move into quarters adjacent to it. Ultimately, the Chinese American women on the Chinatown YWCA board pushed to keep the living quarters racially segregated to protect the women who lived there from anti-Chinese violence.[64] This choice to keep the living quarters separated unfortunately meant that the White women's quarters were the only ones with the private amenities that Morgan intended to include for all the residents, because more funds were allocated to the White residence and community center than the Chinese women's residence. Although the living quarters were segregated, the design of both the Clay Street Center and the Residence set an aesthetic tone that crossed segregation lines that actual women could not. The continuity of architecture between the adjoining buildings anticipated a moment in which the women themselves would not be segregated.

In lieu of social integration, the Chinatown YWCA integrated Chinese design into a Western-style community center and adjoining residence. In McNeill's words about the building, "the infusion of an Eastern aesthetic underscores a dialectic, rather than sheer dominance or oppression, between hegemonic and minority cultures."[65] For example, the south wall of the interior courtyard—part of the White members' section—features glass tiles impressed with

Figure 13. Street view of the Powell Street façade of the Chinatown YWCA. Photograph by Kristen Sheets.

Figure 14. "Cloud lift" detail on the top of the windows facing the courtyard of the Chinatown YWCA Clay Street Center. The tiles in the bottom left corner over the EXIT sign were the same type used to adorn the south wall of the Residence. Photograph by Zoya Brumberg-Kraus.

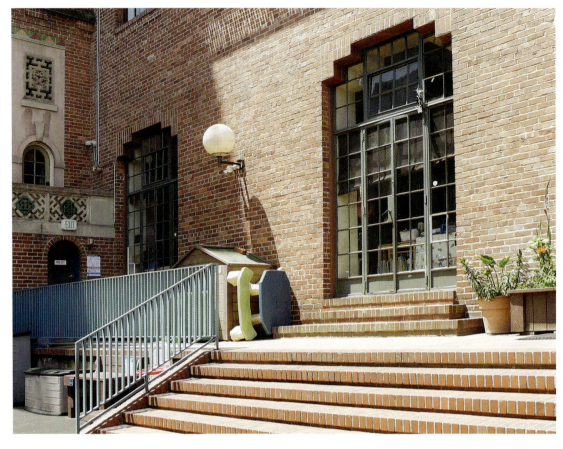

Chinese motifs.[66] The street-level exterior of the White quarters did not incorporate the same Chinese design elements as the Clay Street Center, but both sections of the Residence featured green-tiled eaved roofs and were conjoined by the tower and courtyard (see Figure 11). Yet the reality of creating segregated living quarters was that the conditions of each side of the building reinforced the unequal social status and opportunities of the women. The White women's rooms were designed for single person occupancy, but the Chinese half of the Residence was designed as a shared dormitory with individual bedrooms and shared common spaces. The White women's living quarters offered more privacy and personal space for the occupants. The Chinese living quarters had a shared kitchen, whereas the White living quarters had individual kitchenettes so that the women who lived there could entertain guests. The shared kitchen in the Chinese women's accommodations did not provide any opportunity for the residents to have separate space or private social entertainment (Figure 17).

Though the Residence featured modern amenities and the "luxuries" of aesthetic design and leisure spaces, the disparate living conditions reflected the racial inequality of Chinese and White women in San Francisco. Even as the Chinatown YWCA sought to be a bridge between the Chinese and White worlds in Chinatown and Nob Hill, the complex's design and use also spoke to the limits of those relationships in the interwar decades.

Conclusion

In 1937, five years after the Chinatown YWCA building opened, national YWCA board representative Myra Smith deemed the Chinatown YWCA inadequate for the organization's services. She critiqued the Chinatown chapter's decentralized hierarchy, lack of participation in national YWCA meetings, and lack of conformity to national programs.[67] From Smith's perspective, the Chinatown YWCA's modified program that focused on the needs of Chinese American women negated the overall aims of the organization, even as the Chinatown YWCA did seek to further the national YWCA value of racial integration and assimilation of immigrant cultures into a pluralistic American identity. Her criticism of the chapter was, at least in part, a criticism of the space that housed it. For Smith, the Chinese motifs of the complex, and the minimal Christian education and absence of devotional spaces in the building's design, subtly countered the Anglo-rooted acculturative functions of YWCAs in ethnic communities across the United States.

Yet Morgan's design represented what women in the Chinatown community wanted. The Chinatown chapter leadership wanted to prioritize the services most needed by women in the neighborhood. To that end, the Chinatown YWCA included spaces for English language classes, legal aid, childcare, athletics, Chinese cultural events, and social events. Its design refuted the idea that "American" meant White and European. Instead, its Americanness was expressed through multiculturalism rather than an erasure of ethnic cultural diversity. Morgan and the Chinatown YWCA board of directors' design ascribed symbolic meaning to a space that was already a physical bridge between Chinatown and White San Francisco. The Chinatown YWCA anchors Chinese American women's history within the San Francisco landscape. Today, it houses the Chinese Historical Society of America (CHSA), continuing its function as an educational and cultural space.

The museum was closed to the public when I visited in the midst of the pandemic in 2021, but I was fortunate that Angelo Racelis, visitor service's associate for the CHSA, was able to show me around the building for my research. The room where the Chinatown YWCA's employees socialized after work was now basement bathrooms. The gymnasium was now an exhibition hall. Otherwise, the complex seemed much the same as it was in Morgan's blueprints. Racelis walked me through the closed-off parts of the buildings—the former Chinese women's living quarters and administrative offices. The group kitchen and dormitories were converted to storage spaces for the museum, stuffed with archives and former exhibition materials (see Figure 17).

Figure 15. Dragon mural on the hallway floor of the Chinatown YWCA Clay Street Center. Photograph by Zoya Brumberg-Kraus.

Figure 16. Detail of the gymnasium ceiling in the Chinatown YWCA Clay Street Center, inspired by Chinese rigid frame buildings. Photograph by Zoya Brumberg-Kraus.

The office of the director was emptied but I imagine it retained the appearance of its previous use: the original desk was replaced with a fold out table, but the original built-in wooden shelves

Figure 17. View of the shared kitchen in the Chinese women's section of the Residence, photographed in 2021. This room is now used as storage by the Chinese Historical Society of America. Photograph by Zoya Brumberg-Kraus.

held an old typewriter, some ashtrays, and a photograph of a Chinese American woman in cat's-eye glasses who was perhaps Jane Kwong Lee, the director of the Chinatown YWCA during World War II. Some parts of the Clay Street Center and Chinese women's living quarters are now the Chinatown Community Children's Center, and the former White women's living quarters are housing for seniors. Neither is part of the CHSA, so I could not view the interiors.

The Chinatown YWCA closed in the 1980s, but its history as a living space for Chinese American women remains in the building. As I exited onto Clay Street, the neighborhood seemed somehow more alive than it was a few hours prior. I walked to Sam Wo for a bowl of jook. It was closed for dine-in, but I waited in the out-the-door line for a plastic container of rice porridge and ate it on a park bench in a playground that was getting increasingly busy. Though Chinatown was not as I remembered, its landscape was still animated by the life force of its origins.

AUTHOR BIOGRAPHY

Zoya Brumberg-Kraus is a scholar whose work explores immigrant experience through the built environment. She was recently a research fellow at the Frankel Center for Advanced Judaic Studies at the University of Michigan Ann Arbor for the 2023–24 theme year Jewish Visual Cultures. She holds a PhD in American Studies from the University of Texas at Austin and an MA in Visual and Critical Studies from the School of the Art Institute of Chicago.

ACKNOWLEDGMENTS

I would like to thank the Chinese Historical Society of America (CHSA) for allowing me to explore and photograph the CHSA museum as well as sections of the former Chinatown YWCA buildings that are closed to the public, and Angelo Racelis for guiding me through the buildings. In addition, I would like to thank Kristen Sheets, Bay Area photographer, for helping me with the images. I would also like to acknowledge the Huntington Library for awarding me a short-term research fellowship and access to an expansive library where I conducted much of this research.

NOTES

1. Charlotte Brooks, *Alien Neighbors, Foreign Friends: Asian Americans, Housing, and the Transformation of Urban California* (Chicago: University of Chicago Press, 2013).

2. Paula Lupkin, *Manhood Factories: YMCA Architecture and the Making of Modern Urban Culture* (Minneapolis: University of Minnesota Press, 2010). In *Manhood Factories,* Lupkin explores the transformation of Young Men's Christian Association buildings from Christian male social centers to recreation centers that served broader sections of the community. These YMCA buildings became significant characteristics of urban centers in the early twentieth century, the same time period in which YWCAs became more important to women in American cities—especially immigrant and working-class women. Julia Morgan was in many ways the unofficial YWCA architect of the Pacific Rim in a trend of monumental community buildings shortly after the YMCA architecture became more important to the American urban landscape.

3. Look Tin Eli, "Our New Oriental City— Veritable Fairy Palaces Filled with the Choicest Treasures of the Orient," in *San Francisco: The Metropolis of the West* (San Francisco: Western Press Association, 1910). Look Tin Eli was the public face of the Chinatown-Beautiful movement, and he used the term "Ori-

ental style" to describe the hybrid Chinese and San Franciscan architecture. This term was also used in contemporaneous publications such as *Architect and Engineer* and in vernacular reviews of businesses in San Francisco's Chinatown as well as non-Chinatown spaces that appropriated the style, such as Grauman's Chinese Theatre. Asian eclectic and Chinatown style are other terms sometimes used to describe the Oriental style.

4. Philip P. Choy, *San Francisco Chinatown: A Guide to Its History and Architecture* (San Francisco: City Lights, 2012), 41.

5. Robert S. Becker and Jane Tillis, *Look Tin Eli: The Mendocino Visionary Who Helped Shape the Chinese-American Experience* (Mendocino, Calif.: Kelley House Museum, 2021), 38.

6. Kenneth Marcus and Yong Chen, "Inside and Outside Chinatown: Chinese Elites in Exclusion Era California," *Pacific Historical Review* 80, no. 3 (August 2011): 371.

7. L. Eva Armentrout Ma, *Hometown Chinatown: A History of Oakland's Chinese Community, 1852–1995* (New York: Garland Publishing, Inc., 2000), 67.

8. Raymond Rast, "The Cultural Politics of Tourism in San Francisco's Chinatown, 1882–1917," *Pacific Historical Review* 76, no. 1 (February 2007): 33.

9. Eli, "Our New Oriental City."

10. Eli, "Our New Oriental City."

11. Jean Moon Liu, *Lew Hing: A Family Portrait* (Oakland, Calif.: Janus Book Publishers, 1987).

12. Becker and Tillis, *Look Tin Eli,* 49.

13. Liu, *Lew Hing,* 13.

14. Choy, *San Francisco Chinatown,* 44–45.

15. "Some of the Recent Work of T. Paterson Ross, Architect, and A.W. Burgren, Engineer," *Architect and Engineer* 31, no. 1 (November 1912): 47.

16. "The Work of T. Paterson Ross and A.W. Burgren," *Architect and Engineer* 13, no. 1 (May 1908): 35.

17. Eiliesh Tuffy and Julia Moore, "Review and Comment on 30 Otis Street Preservation Alternatives for Draft EIR Case No. 2015–010013ENV," report to the Architectural Review Committee for the Historic Preservation Commission, San Francisco Planning Department (October 25, 2017), 51.

18. "The Work of T. Paterson Ross and A.W. Burgren," 35.

19. Choy, *San Francisco Chinatown,* 45.

20. Eli, "Our New Oriental City," 68.

21. Christopher Yip, "San Francisco's Chinatown: An Architectural and Urban History," PhD diss., University of California, Berkeley, 1985, 26.

22. Eli, "Our New Oriental City," 68.

23. Ellen Wu, "Deghettoizing Chinatown: Race and Space in Postwar America," in *Race and Retail: Consumption across the Color Line,* ed. Mia Bay and Ann Fabian (New Brunswick, N.J.: Rutgers University Press, 2015), 142.

24. Kim Fahlstedt, *Chinatown Film Culture: The Appearance of Cinema in San Francisco's Chinese Neighborhood* (New Brunswick, N.J.: Rutgers University Press, 2020), 54.

25. Wu, "Deghettoizing Chinatown," 142.

26. Eli, "Our New Oriental City," 68.

27. Marcus and Chen, "Inside and Outside Chinatown," 370.

28. Rast, "The Cultural Politics of Tourism," 33.

29. Ma, *Hometown Chinatown,* 67.

30. Becker and Tillis, *Look Tin Eli,* 32.

31. Selma Siew Li Bidlingmaier, "Spaces of Alterity and Temporal Permanence: The Case of San Francisco's and New York's Chinatowns," in *Selling EthniCity,* ed. Olaf Kaltmeier (London: Routledge, 2011), 281.

32. Bay Area News Group, "Exhibit Offers History of Miss Chinatown USA," *East Bay Times* (March 30, 2007).

33. Edward Said, *Orientalism* (New York: Vintage Books, 1979), 234.

34. Karen McNeill, personal notes from the San Francisco YWCA minutes, 1928, Papers of the San Francisco YWCA, YWCA of San Francisco and Marin, San Francisco, California [hereafter cited as "YWCA minutes"].

35. Judy Yung, *Unbound Feet: A Social History of Chinese Women in San Francisco* (Berkeley: University of California Press, 1995), 95.

36. Karen McNeill, "Women Who Build: Julia Morgan & Women's Institutions," *California History* 89, no. 3 (2012): 59.

37. Choy, *San Francisco Chinatown,* 184.

38. McNeill, "Women Who Build," 59.

39. Yung, *Unbound Feet,* 37.

40. Yung, *Unbound Feet,* 93.

41. McNeill, "Women Who Build," 62.

42. Judy Yung, *Unbound Voices: A Documentary History of Chinese Women in San Francisco* (Berkeley: University of California Press, 1999), 225.

43. McNeill, "Women Who Build," 66.

44. Yong Chen, *Chinese San Francisco, 1850–1943: A Trans-Pacific Community* (Palo Alto, Calf.: Stanford University Press, 2000).

45. Yung, *Unbound Feet*, 95.

46. Karen McNeill, "Julia Morgan: Gender, Architecture, and Professional Style," *Pacific Historical Review* 76, no. 2 (May 2007): 257.

47. YWCA minutes, 1928; Yung, *Unbound Feet*.

48. Choy, *San Francisco Chinatown*, 182; YWCA minutes, 1928.

49. Rose Chew, "Manifestations of Modern Influences on Second-Generation Chinese (1930)" in *Unbound Voices: A Documentary History of Chinese Women in San Francisco*, ed. Judy Yung (Berkeley: University of California Press, 1999), 263.

50. Julia Flynn Siler, *The White Devil's Daughters: The Women Who Fought Slavery in San Francisco Chinatown* (New York: Knopf, 2019), 75.

51. Sarah Holmes Boutelle, *Julia Morgan: Architect* (New York: Abbeville Press Publishers, 1988), 64.

52. Boutelle, *Julia Morgan*, 64.

53. Interview with Walter Steilberg, "Julia Morgan Architectural History Project Interviews," vol. 1, transcript, Bancroft Library, Regional Oral History Office, University of California, Berkeley.

54. McNeill, "Women Who Build," 62.

55. McNeill, "Julia Morgan," 230.

56. McNeill, "Julia Morgan," 240.

57. Shirley Contreras, "Dorothy Wormser Was the First Female Jewish Architect in the West," *Santa Maria Times* (June 1, 2008).

58. Victoria Kastner, *Julia Morgan: An Intimate Portrait of the Trailblazing Architect* (San Francisco: Chronicle Books, 2022), 184.

59. Sachi Oka, "Sachi Oka: Julia Morgan's Housekeeper," interview by John Horn and Ted Moreno in *Oral History Project* (San Simeon, Calif.: Hearst San Simeon State Historical Monument Archives, 1995).

60. McNeill, "Women Who Build," 64.

61. Boutelle, *Julia Morgan*, 118.

62. Boutelle, *Julia Morgan*, 118.

63. Choy, *San Francisco Chinatown*, 181.

64. YWCA minutes, 1928.

65. McNeill, "Women Who Build," 64.

66. McNeill, "Women Who Build," 64.

67. McNeill, "Women Who Build," 66.

TESSA EVANS

Political Landscapes and Rival Cultural Landscapes in Spanish Louisiana

Antoine Sarrasin and la Cyprière

ABSTRACT

This article examines the life of Antoine Sarrasin—an important yet understudied figure in early American history—and his role in organizing the 1795 Pointe Coupée rebellion to abolish slavery in Spanish Louisiana. Proposing the idea of rival cultural landscapes created by freed and enslaved people that deliberately challenged the political landscapes shaped by their Spanish rulers, this article traces the creation of a particular Black geographic experience and analyzes how Sarrasin creatively utilized a common feature of Spanish plantations—the cypress swamp (*la cyprière*)—to secretly plan an elaborate, multiracial rebellion influenced by his knowledge of Atlantic revolutionary activity. His intimate understanding of the cypress swamps reveals a historical familiarity and mastery of the natural world that many enslaved and free people of African descent created during the eighteenth and nineteenth centuries. This article contributes to current interdisciplinary scholarship that maps Black geographic experiences throughout the diaspora and recovers routes and paths that enslaved and free people of African descent "invisibly" marked on the landscape to contest White geographic domination. Though many others acted similarly to Sarrasin, their stories have been lost to the modern archive. Finding ways to creatively and critically engage with the archive to recover the stories of those like Sarrasin is one way we can tell a more inclusive history of early America.

On an early spring day in 1795, Antoine Sarrasin—an important yet understudied figure from early America—walked on a path to the port along the False and Mississippi Rivers, where he often worked loading and unloading cargo as an enslaved man living on one of Julien Poydras's Pointe Coupée plantations, located northwest of present-day Baton Rouge, Louisiana. While on the dock, he met two free men of African descent who were passing through from New Orleans to Natchez. According to his court testimony, these two men told Sarrasin that the king of Spain had freed all of the slaves in the Louisiana territory, and that he, Sarrasin, would receive freedom soon.[1] Hearing this news, he walked back along the path of the False River to the slave quarters on the Poydras plantation. There, he talked with

other enslaved individuals, who informed him this was a rumor. Undeterred, Sarrasin went back to his cabin, where he began to plan his own immediate end to slavery, a rebellion that would ultimately fail.

As we will see in his court case, Sarrasin continued to discuss, plan, and organize a rebellion throughout the early months of 1795. He chose to organize this rebellion in *la cyprière,* the meandering cypress swamps located in the back of the former French, now Spanish, plantations along the navigable rivers. It was the perfect place. There, he was able to form a community of revolutionaries made up of enslaved individuals from neighboring plantations, free people of African descent, White men, and even Indigenous Tunica women who worked planting corn near *la cyprière.* Antoine Sarrasin demonstrated that he knew how to use this landscape.

The cypress swamp provides an example of the crucial role that the physical environment and landscape played in events in early American history. The physical environment, paired with Sarrasin's intimate knowledge of the plantation landscape, enabled him to plan a revolution. He had direct access to networks of information and knowledge, including the aforementioned rumor that spread throughout the Atlantic basin, as well as news of the slave uprising unfolding in Saint-Domingue in present-day Haiti beginning in 1791. But without his knowledge of the cypress swamps in the Pointe Coupée plantation zone, Sarrasin would not have been able to bring together a community of people who were committed to executing a carefully planned rebellion. He and the others planned to steal weapons and ammunition from the plantation storehouses, set the plantations on fire, and kill the Whites living in Pointe Coupée Parish. They could then live freely and liberate themselves from the confines of Atlantic slavery. Sarrasin determined that the cypress swamp was out of the gaze and surveillance of the White population and was considered inaccessible to them, yet it was navigable and even well known to the enslaved community and others who lived on the peripheries of Spanish Louisiana plantations.

By meeting in a secretive, difficult-to-access space, Sarrasin was able to bring together a multiracial community of revolutionaries who were able to plan this rebellion in great detail. Sarrasin cultivated this intimate knowledge and mastery of the cypress swamps and knew the navigable paths to the False and Mississippi Rivers after years of working in this particular landscape. Ironically, this knowledge, which was an unintended consequence for the French and Spanish slave masters who forced the laborers to work in these spaces, would eventually be used as a revolutionary space in an attempt to overthrow them.[2]

The life and actions of Antoine Sarrasin (1757–95) have not been reexamined in great detail since Gwendolyn Midlo Hall's monumental 1992 book *Africans in Colonial Louisiana: The Development of Afro-Creole Culture in the Eighteenth Century.*[3] Furthermore, no historians have specifically examined the landscape and environment in an analysis of the rebellion in Pointe Coupée. This article accomplishes several goals. I add to the burgeoning historiography that combines cultural landscape studies and slavery studies to better understand the geographic materialities of slavery in the Atlantic world, and I also examine how enslaved and free people of African descent created and mapped Black geographies and spaces within a colonial context.[4] This requires a conversation with interdisciplinary scholars Katherine McKittrick, Stephanie Camp, and Rashauna Johnson, who incorporate geography, the environment, and the physical and cultural landscape to show how enslaved people interacted with, shaped, and manipulated the physical world and occupied spaces that were shared by colonial inhabitants, resulting in the creation of new rival geographies and landscapes. Their work challenges the belief that enslaved and free people of African descent understood and moved through the physical environment in the same way as their White counterparts.[5] Second, this article adds to the historiographical work among interdisciplinary scholars who incorporate the environment and physical spaces to critically understand larger historical forces such as colonialism, slavery, resistance, rebellion, and liberation. Scholars Monique Allewaert and Jessica George look at the writings of Southerners and visitors to the American South and Caribbean who describe the swamplands, and they both find that these were contested spaces that challenged colonial rule by enslaved and free Black individuals.[6]

Antoine Sarrasin occupied a unique space in early America as an Afro-Native man with European ancestry. He lived on a large indigo and sugar plantation in Spanish Louisiana with a Black majority. Unfortunately, in his lifetime, social and political changes brought by a new Spanish presence in Louisiana beginning in 1762 thwarted the hope of an enslaved person of Afro-Native ancestry who endeavored to use Spanish legal measures to gain his freedom. He lived in a time of great turmoil and change in the Atlantic world and Spanish Louisiana. Afro-Native interactions in the Louisiana territory were complex, and these interactions, made manifest in the person of Antoine Sarrasin, caused concern and paranoia among European planters and Spanish officials. Spanish rule brought changes to the structure of slavery, including the prohibition of slavery for Native Americans, which led to an increase in Native Americans suing for and winning their freedom. While Spanish laws changed how slavery looked in Spanish Louisiana, French and Spanish planters were keeping abreast of events in the Atlantic world while trying to keep their grasp on slavery on their own plantations in Louisiana. This political and social context helps to clarify the circumstances that greatly influenced Antoine Sarrasin, and helps to answer why he felt disillusioned and further marginalized.

Landscapes in the Louisiana territory, beginning with French, Spanish, and subsequent Anglo-American occupations, were permanently marked by extensions of colonial control, thereby delineating political power and social stratification. These political landscapes often served to curtail or limit how certain people could move through a particular space, and even limit how an individual could make a decision about mobility based on physical barriers or other factors; for example, fences or walls sought to keep certain people in, and certain people out.[7] In a political landscape, those with traditional forms of power (White European males in this context) shaped and manipulated the physical landscape to inscribe and naturalize their authority and prestige. A plantation provides a clear example of a political landscape. On antebellum plantations, slave owners sought to control the mobility of their enslaved workers and used the physical plantation to execute their goals of control and surveillance. Slave owners decided where the slave cabins were built and where the slaves would work. The built environment was designed to surveille the mobility of the enslaved.[8]

Regardless of these measures to control people's movements, historians, geographers, and anthropologists find that people were still able to create alternative rival cultural landscapes to both evade and challenge these articulations of power on their respective political landscapes.[9] Looking for instances in the historical record in which marginalized people, like Sarrasin, challenged and created their own rival geographies or used their geographic literacy to their own advantage helps us see how people without traditional forms of power challenged political control on their own terms using their own methods.

Antoine Sarrasin's rebellion transformed the cypress swamps of Louisiana plantations into a rival cultural landscape, one that deliberately challenged the Spanish political landscape. The Spanish government responded to Sarrasin's actions by making a political statement on the very same *cyprière*. In executing the rebellion's conspirators and placing their heads on pikes on paths along the swamps of the False and Mississippi Rivers—including the head of Antoine Sarrasin—Spanish leaders ended the rebellion, extinguished further plans for subsequent uprisings, and reasserted their claims to power. We can understand the physical landscapes of *la cyprière* in Louisiana as spaces of competing power: political landscapes created by Spanish rulers, and rival cultural landscapes created by the actions of freed and enslaved people like Antoine Sarrasin.

Slavery, Freedom, and Identity in the Lower Mississippi River Valley

Antoine Sarrasin found himself inextricably bound to the political and social forces at play in eighteenth-century Pointe Coupée, Louisiana. French settlers founded Pointe Coupée in 1717, and it functioned as a coveted trading post along the Mississippi River halfway between Natchez and New Orleans. The French founded the settlement along the False River, which was a channel of the Mississippi, but in 1722 the river changed its course and the False River was cut off, hence the name Pointe Coupée, which the Spanish translated literally as Punta Cortada, "cutoff point" (Figure 1).

The area around the False and Mississippi Rivers had a powerful Native American presence, and the French settlement was built close to a Tunica village. The Tunica chose to ally with the French to enhance trading.[10] The remote Pointe Coupée trading post witnessed a surge of French and Native American violence following the Natchez massacre of 1729, during which the Tunica

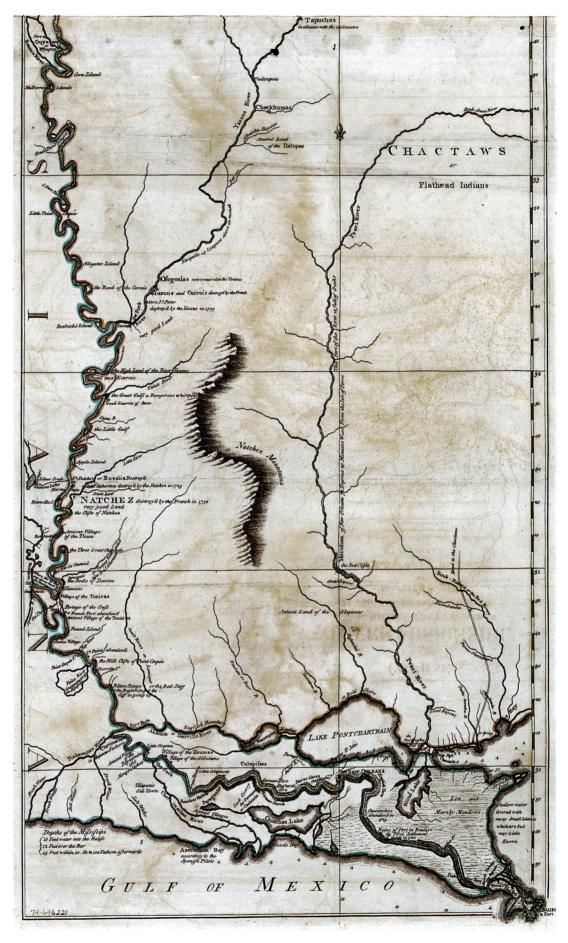

Figure 1. Map of the Mississippi River, showing Pointe Coupée, Louisiana, and the circular-shaped False River upstream from New Orleans at bottom left. The landscape surrounding the False River was swamp filled with cypress trees, known as *la cyprière*. Detail of map, Lieut. Ross and Robert Sayer, *Course of the river Mississippi, from the Balise to Fort Chartres; taken on an expedition to the Illinois, in the latter end of the year* (London: Printed for Robt. Sayer, 1765). Courtesy of the Library of Congress.

allied with the French and waged battles against the remnants of the Natchez tribe. Historian Gwendolyn Midlo Hall found that there were frequent raids at Pointe Coupée from roaming Chickasaw bands and remnants of the Natchez people, who were seeking refuge in Louisiana after their villages were destroyed in 1729. Like other colonial settlements in the borderlands, Pointe Coupée was a violent, unstable, disputed Native American and European borderland.[11]

Adding to this tension was the growing number of enslaved Africans who were forced to work on tobacco and indigo plantations that now extended farther into the swampy landscape. At Pointe Coupée, enslaved people outnumbered Europeans, and racial mixing among Natives, people of African descent, and Europeans led to a diverse population of mulattos (people of African and European descent) and *grifs* (people of Afro-Native descent).[12] Manumissions during both French and Spanish occupations led to a high population of free people of African and Afro-Native descent. Hall also found that French and Spanish men often recognized their offspring with enslaved women through manumissions and gifts of money, though this did not happen for Antoine Sarrasin.[13] Even with their freedom, people of mixed ancestry often occupied a precarious position in society, where they were considered neither enslaved nor free.

Unfortunately, like many enslaved people, not much is known about the origins of Antoine Sarrasin, though some records exist about his father—also named Antoine, called *père* (father) but with a last name spelled Sarrassin—which help place his son's story into historical context. We know that Antoine Sarrassin *père* was a French resident of Pointe Coupée, and that his brother, François Sarrassin, served as a Quapaw interpreter at the Spanish Arkansas Post farther upriver. We know Antoine *père* and François were brothers since several documents exist that contain both of their names and establish their relationship.[14] Their father, Nicolas Sarrazin, was a fur trader in New Orleans.[15] He lived with his wife, Anne Rolland, and their three children, including the eldest son, Antoine, middle son, François, and youngest son, Michel, who were

born between 1721 and 1727.[16] Their father died in 1727, leaving Anne with an estate; she remarried twice and moved to the Natchez Post in the 1730s. François took a position as a French cadet and interpreter at the Arkansas Post, where he fathered children with Quapaw women, including one son, Saracen, who became leader of one of the Quapaw tribes during the era of Quapaw removal in the early nineteenth century.[17] This Saracen was remembered as a friend of the French settlers in present-day southeastern Arkansas and even a hero after he supposedly saved French children from a Chickasaw war party.[18] The life of this Saracen—the child of a French man and Indigenous woman in the colonial borderlands—varies greatly from that of his cousin Antoine Sarrasin, leader of the failed Pointe Coupée rebellion, demonstrating the widely diverse experiences for children produced in these cross-cultural encounters in the French and Spanish borderlands in the eighteenth century.

French planter Antoine Sarrassin *père* lived among the elite at Pointe Coupée, within a landscape of slavery. His social status is conveyed in various court cases in the French Superior Council (1714–69) and Spanish Judicial Records (1769–1803). In 1748, Antoine Sarrassin *père* was a witness for a contract between Sieur Meuillion and his brother, Pierre Daspit (called Saint Amant), for the sale of an enslaved woman, Lizette.[19] In 1762, he served as witness for an exchange of land and an enslaved woman between a Jeanne Rabalay and a Mr. Guichanduc.[20] He served as a witness for a contract made by Claude Trénonay during the settling of an estate in Pointe Coupée and again regarding a house in New Orleans.[21] As we shall see later, Trénonay was a large-scale planter who was murdered by an enslaved man in 1791, the same year a slave insurrection sparked the Haitian Revolution.

Not only was Antoine Sarrassin *père* himself a slave owner, but we know of his intimate relationships with enslaved people, as he fathered Antoine Sarrasin *fils* (son) with an enslaved woman of African and Native descent named Marie-Jeanne.[22] Antoine Sarrassin *père*, his wife Marie Colon, and his brother Michel often engaged in the buying and selling of enslaved people in the Pointe

Coupée district. For instance, Antoine *père* and Michel bought an enslaved woman of African descent in 1744 from a Madame Pierremont, presumably while he was living in Pointe Coupée.[23] No major records of Sarrassin's plantation (like the plantation plats cited later in this article) survive, perhaps because neither he nor his heirs were alive when these were issued by Spanish royal surveyors in the 1780s and 1790s. Perhaps he had no legal heirs since he never recognized Antoine *fils* as his legitimate son. After his death, his widow, Marie Colon, bought and sold slaves, indicating that his household and plantation remained in her control. In 1766 she bought Hector and Jupiter, perhaps peers and friends of Antoine Sarrasin *fils,* and later in that year she bought a "healthy negro valued at 1500 livres," whose name was not listed, from a Madame Marie Richaume.[24]

While we do not know if Antoine Sarrasin *fils* was ever owned by his slave-owner father, we do know that he was owned by Julien Poydras, a wealthy French planter and politician who owned several plantations and hundreds of slaves in the Pointe Coupée district.[25] While his cousin Saracen, of the Arkansas Post, was of European and Native descent, Antoine Sarrasin had French, Indigenous, and African ancestry. His mother, Marie-Jeanne, was an enslaved woman of both African and Native ancestry. She sued for her freedom based on her Native ancestry and won that freedom suit, based on the fact that her mother was a Native woman. (Her mother and Antoine Sarrasin *fils*'s grandmother, Thérèse Sauvage [*sic*], was enslaved but given her freedom in 1769 when Spain outlawed Native slavery in the Louisiana territory.)[26]

Sarrasin's ancestry illustrates the close connections between people of African descent and Native Americans in Louisiana, founded largely on the fact that both groups of people were enslaved by French settlers. Holding both Natives and people of African descent in slavery led to intimate connections between the two groups, which also led to a new class of people known as *grifs,* whose status as enslaved or free became murkier as the eighteenth century wore on, and became an issue for slaveholders. Sarrasin's an-

cestry as an Afro-Indigenous European man put him in a particularly precarious position in Spanish Louisiana, and looking at these connections among Natives and people of African descent helps us contextualize and better understand his story and his dedication to securing his freedom.

Native slavery was widespread in the Lower Mississippi River Valley. Although the Spanish governors of the Louisiana territory sought to uphold Spain's laws against it, French and Spanish settlers in Pointe Coupée bought and sold enslaved Native people throughout the eighteenth century. Enforcement of the law was difficult in practice and a low priority for the Spanish judiciary.[27] Native slavery was so prevalent in the territory that even people who owned few material possessions bought and owned Native American slaves. For instance, in 1737 a small-scale planter named Antoine Beauregard was killed near Baton Rouge. While settling his small estate at Pointe Coupée, the affidavit listed that he "has neither cattle, nor clothes, nor effects . . . in his possession, except two old shirts, a worn out pair of breeches, an Indian woman, a crock containing about four pitchers of oil, and forty pounds of tobacco."[28] Even a relatively poor man, as indicated by the possessions in his estate, was able to own a Native woman, whom he most likely held as a concubine. A French hunter living on the Arkansas River stipulated in his will in 1767 that he wanted to free two Native slaves and their two children "in gratitude for their services rendered him." That this man, Michel Allemand, was able to own two enslaved Native people yet had few other material possessions signals the low status of these people.[29]

We know that intimacies between people of African descent and Native Americans created legal challenges for Spanish lawmakers and European planters, who viewed these intimate connections as a threat to their hegemony. Spanish lawmakers saw firsthand the problems surrounding enslaved people of African descent and enslaved Native Americans living and working together on the same plantations, from creating informal trade networks to running away.[30]

Race was so fluid in Spanish Louisiana that not even enslavers could keep track of the status of those they enslaved, and certainly could not make this distinction based on physical appearances. Consequently, it is no surprise that in court cases Antoine Sarrasin *fils* is recorded as a mulatto, though he referred to himself as a Creole.[31] In another case, during the settlement of an estate in the Illinois territory in 1791, Manuel Bourguignon sued Dame Louise Perthuis, having found out that the enslaved man he had bought from her had already been granted his freedom twenty-five years prior. Dame Perthuis had claimed the man to be a mulatto but "it was discovered that said mulatto was an Indian, belonging to a race free of servitude."[32] Whether this unnamed enslaved man was really a *grif* or a mulatto is unknown; however, in this particular case the enslaved man was granted his freedom because the courts were able to find his previous freedom suit.[33]

The existence of a free Black population in the Lower Mississippi River Valley added to anxiety over slavery, freedom, and identity in the region. Gwendolyn Midlo Hall estimated that there were a total of two hundred free and enslaved people of mixed European and African descent living at Pointe Coupée in 1769, and fifty-five free people of African descent (without any racial mixing with Europeans) by 1803, although these numbers are not wholly accurate since many census records from the Spanish period at Pointe Coupée are missing.[34] These freed individuals—some of African ancestry, some of European and African ancestry, and others of Native and African ancestry—would have had a variety of jobs at the remote settlement. For instance, in 1762, a free "mulatto" named Louis made a contract with Pierre Ricard and Francois Allain, who were storekeepers at Pointe Coupée. These Frenchmen wanted to start a "cattle breeding settlement" and hired Louis "to manage the said business and agree to give him one-tenth of all breeding cows in compensation for his labor and care."[35] Antoine Sarrasin *fils* may have seen these free people of African descent working, being paid a wage, and living with a modicum of freedom.

Indeed, Antoine Sarrasin firmly believed that his identity as an Afro-Native could bring about his immediate freedom, which is why he used the Spanish courts to sue for his freedom, citing the fact that his grandmother was Native, his mother was an Afro-Native, and his father was French. Somewhat surprisingly, Sarrasin did not win this suit for freedom.[36] His mother, Marie-Jeanne, cited her son in her freedom testimony, stating he was a *metizo* (born to a French father). Sarrasin's owner, Julien Poydras, testified against Sarrasin, stating he was the property of Poydras's estate (it is unclear when Poydras purchased Sarrasin). Poydras even petitioned Governor Francisco Louis Héctor, the Baron de Carondelet, in 1794 to end the freeing of Native slaves, since he, like other French planters, thought this policy was slowly eroding his power as a slave owner.[37] Antoine Sarrasin's failed freedom suit left him disillusioned with the system, perhaps indicating why he and others endeavored to destroy the system of slavery completely and immediately, on their own terms.[38] Sarrasin's disappointment with the limitations and vicissitudes of the Spanish legal system led to his involvement in a radical plan, and these political events led him to take his liberty "by force" (*ils étaient décidé à prendre leur liberté par force*).[39]

Rival Cultural Landscapes and Rebellion in Spanish Louisiana

The physical environment in which Sarrasin lived and worked radically aided his planning of a rebellion. Sarrasin occupied a particular space in Spanish Louisiana. According to interdisciplinary scholars, a physical landscape can be inscribed with different meanings and uses based on who, specifically, is engaging with that landscape.[40] In a colonial setting, we find two different types of landscapes: a political landscape and a rival cultural landscape.

Plantations are perhaps the best example of a political landscape in a colonial setting. Planters in colonial America and the Atlantic world carefully designed plantations to visibly demonstrate their wealth, power, and prestige. These political landscapes were processional, meaning specific people were supposed to move through the landscape differently, as a nineteenth-century painting by Father Joseph M. Paret of a plantation near

New Orleans illustrates (Figure 2).[41] French and Spanish colonists moved through the plantation in an organized, hierarchal way. They walked down the carefully contrived road or path to the planter's home, seeing only what the planter wanted them to see: gardens, formal parks, lines of trees, organized and tidy dependencies. The planter's home was at the center of this processional landscape: all roads and paths led to him. Enslaved people were to move through the plantation spaces differently, using the paths behind the big house to get from place to place instead of the formal paths or roads.[42] The plantation served as a physical manifestation of colonial power and authority.[43] However, the planter was unable to control all aspects of the plantation, including *la cyprière*.

In spite of the endeavors of planters to inscribe their power on the physical landscape, this power unfolded unequally on the ground, which resulted in a landscape etched with meaning based on human interactions.[44] By using the landscape as a category of historical analysis, we can see how the planter's power over his physical plantation was tenuous and often challenged by those who also occupied these plantation spaces. Enslaved people changed and used the landscapes within the periphery of the plantation—in the case of Louisiana plantations, the backswamps—to exert a modicum of control and even create some power over their own space, and to challenge the power of the planter on the same disputed landscape. Archaeologist Suzanne Spencer-Wood argued that enslaved people challenged planter hegemony by using parts of the plantation landscape "in ways that were not intended by their owners."[45] Nowhere is this clearer than on the plantations at Pointe Coupée in the 1790s.

Figure 2. An 1859 watercolor painting by Father Joseph M. Paret of the Hermitage Plantation located in St. Charles, Louisiana, twelve miles west of New Orleans and about a hundred miles southeast of Pointe Coupée. This painting shows the orderly plantation landscape, with the slave quarters on the periphery near the water. Note how enslaved and White people would have walked through and experienced this space differently in an example of a processional landscape. Courtesy of Jay D. Edwards.

The term "rival cultural landscape" builds on the ideas of rival geographies and geographic literacy proposed by two historians of slavery, Stephanie Camp and Rashauna Johnson. Camp coined the term "rival geography" to describe the spaces created by enslaved women to bypass the prescribed spaces on plantations and to carve out spaces for themselves. According to Camp, the rival geographies were "alternative ways of knowing and using plantation and southern space that conflicted with planters' ideals and demands."[46] While she writes that slave masters wanted to control the mobility of enslaved people by creating a "geography of containment," Camp argues that enslaved people sometimes experienced movement and mobility that rivaled this containment. Adding to the historiography of slavery and space, Johnson's argument centers on how historians conceptualize mobility when discussing slavery. Johnson demonstrates how enslaved people in New Orleans experienced unprecedented mobility by accompanying their masters to disparate places in the Atlantic world. This mobility led to the creation of "geographic literacy," which is a term she employs to describe knowledge about the physical and social world that enslaved people garnered through these experiences.[47]

Literary scholar Monique Allewaert discusses the role of swamps in colonial literary traditions, and in particular travel narratives throughout the Atlantic world. She argues that swamplands compromised the order and productivity found within Atlantic plantations. These spaces incited fear and anxiety among White residents, whereas self-emancipating runaway slaves known as maroons viewed these swamplands as safe from control and oversight.[48] My research builds on the work of Camp and Johnson by applying their theories of rival geographies and geographic literacy to understand the actions of Antoine Sarrasin and his collaborators. Sarassin created a rival cultural landscape within the cypress swamps of Pointe Coupée based on his geographic literacy as an enslaved man. This action supports Allewaert's interpretation of swamps as revolutionary spaces, which marginalized groups in the Atlantic world used for political and individual gain. In this process, she argues, some of these swamps became "Africanized" spaces, at the same time Europeans were endeavoring to transform these spaces into profitable plantations of the Atlantic world.[49]

In the Louisiana territory, we can literally see French colonization by looking at the landscape. We know by the physical changes to the landscape that it was originally a French and not a Spanish or British colony. The actual method in which French plantations in the Louisiana territory were carved out of the physical landscape created backswamps in the Louisiana territory, including plantation complexes at Pointe Coupée.[50] Colonial French plantations in North America and throughout the French empire were long and narrow, so that each landowner had access to a navigable waterway and usually a natural levee at the back of their property for more efficient travel and shipping of goods, called a backswamp.[51] Plantation plats from Pointe Coupée show these backswamps at the end of individual plantations. In Pointe Coupée, Joseph DeCuir's 1802 land grant backs up to the False River (Rio Fausse), with a variety of cypress swamps, bayous, and small bodies of water listed on the surveyor's plat (Figure 3).[52]

These backswamps and small ports and bays along a river such as the Mississippi tended to be surrounded by spaces of water that "trail[ed] off into cypress swamps and woodlands" according to Hall.[53] Plantations in the French and subsequent Spanish Louisiana territory included the cypress swamp, since Spaniards left these plantation layouts intact. According to eighteenth-century European cartographers, these cypress swamps were "inaccessible" spaces, and were labeled as such on plantation plats at Pointe Coupée. Seven extant plantation plats from the late eighteenth century illustrate these cypress swamps and bodies of water within the plantation complex at Pointe Coupée. For example, an 1803 plat of a plantation belonging to Francisco Allain illustrates how his plantation was located along the Mississippi River and Bayou Sara. The 1795 plat of David Lamar and Luis Alston illustrates their land stretching back to the Mississippi River, as does the 1801 plat of Luis Richet.[54]

The importance of these "inaccessible spaces,"

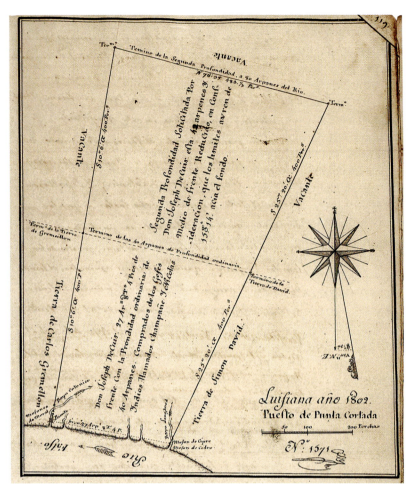

Figure 3. Joseph DeCuir's 1802 plantation plat in Pointe Coupée, showing the narrow plantation landscape with access to the Rio Fausse (False River) and swamps (bottom left-hand corner). From the Pintado Papers, mss 890, 1223, Louisiana and Lower Mississippi Valley Collections, Louisiana State University Libraries, Baton Rouge.

sometimes referred to as "dismal swamps" by Europeans, cannot be overstated. Based on extant court records from the French Superior Council and the Spanish Judicial Records, enslaved people and free people of African descent used cypress swamps in acts of resistance. Indeed, these court cases highlight that the cypress swamps were problematic and dangerous areas where colonial control remained tenuous. Allewaert argues that swamps were problematic to colonial officials in the Caribbean and Atlantic world: "there was perhaps no space more paradigmatically tropical and more threatening to colonials than the swamps . . . [since] they compromised the order and productivity of imperial ventures from explorations to plantations."[55] She further explains that swamps were difficult for colonial armies to maneuver, and even more difficult for cartographers to adequately portray in maps.[56] Therefore, they were the ideal space for enslaved and free people of African descent to make their own in colonial Louisiana. Regarding those enslaved on the plantations of the Atlantic world, historians have long noted the frequency of runaways and self-liberated people of African descent creating maroon communities in swamplands, on mountains, and in other peripheral locations out of view of Europeans.[57] In Louisiana, the swamplands offered the most protection and secrecy.

Even before Antoine Sarrasin's revolutionary actions, we see the creation of a rival cultural landscape within the plantation swamps in several instances at Pointe Coupée. In French and Spanish Louisiana, these swamps offered spaces for enslaved people to engage in acts of resistance, from the small scale—meeting secretly, engaging in the trading and selling of goods, hiding out temporarily—to the larger scale—planning revolts and establishing maroon communities. Such was the case in southern Louisiana at Bas du Fleuve east of New Orleans, one of the few successful maroon communities in North America of up to fifty fugitive slaves that was so well organized and powerful that it required Spanish military intervention to dismantle in 1784.[58]

Wealthy tobacco planter Claudio Trénonay's plat of his large estate from 1787 showed how his plantation went directly back to Bayou Sara, a tributary of the Mississippi River, with illustrations of the cypress swamps connecting the river with the bayou (Figure 4). Trénonay, the man for whom Antoine Sarassin's father had served as a witness on his contracts, was murdered in 1791 by one of his enslaved men, a runaway who had been living in the cypress swamps on Trénonay's plantation in Pointe Coupée for three weeks.[59] This self-emancipating runaway, named Latulipe Ibo (indicating his origins in West Africa), turned the cypress swamp into a rival cultural landscape on his master's plantation. Latulipe hid in the cypress swamp and stockpiled weapons so that he could plan a well-orchestrated attack on his master. The Spanish judiciary responded to this bold assertion of power by executing and dismembering Latulipe Ibo, and placing his body parts on posts throughout Trénonay's plantation—the very same demonstration of political power that occurred with the execution and dismemberment of Antoine Sarrasin on the very same landscape.

There are many extant examples of enslaved people using swamps to evade colonial control in the eighteenth century. In 1737, the French Superior Council examined a runaway slave, Geula, who had "marooned in the cypress tract" on his owner's plantation.[60] In 1748, Francois, an enslaved man, was charged with theft and *marronage* (running away permanently). He recounted his experiences using the cypress swamps on his master's plantation to hide successfully for several weeks, thus illustrating how enslaved people used the swamps for acts of resistance.[61] During the Spanish occupation of the Louisiana territory, an enslaved man named Bizago was imprisoned for marronage, and his owner claimed him missing for nearly four years before he was apprehended. Bizago testified that he lived in the woods and swamps between various plantations and supported himself by "killing rabbits which he sold" to several people.[62] He was accused of stealing goods from other enslaved people and selling the goods, including to another maroon, Louis, who also lived in the "Cypress Grove" where he had set up temporary housing.[63] Bizago had an obvious knowledge of the Louisiana landscape. In the trial, he said that he found a canoe and filled it with stolen goods, and the Spanish judiciary further explained that he "had taken a small canoe . . . on the other side of the river . . . setting it adrift . . . to have even built a hut to hide some goods."[64] He was able to survive and carve out a space for himself on the plantation landscapes of southern Louisiana—perhaps even "Africanizing" the space, as articulated by Allewaert—and the fact that he did so for four years is a testament to his knowledge of this particular environment.[65]

Cypress swamps were also spaces of collaboration with Native American groups and individuals. Native American and African slaves sometimes ran away together, thus creating more anxiety for planters. For instance, in 1727 a runaway Native slave was accused not only of marronage, but of "enticing an Indian slave girl, belonging to Mr. Saint Amand, to rob her mistress and run away with him, to join some fugitive slaves who had set up a village."[66] This court case does not mention where Amand's plantation was located. However, an extant plantation plat from M. Alexandre Daspie de Saint Amant survives, which places this plantation near Valenzuela, Louisiana (a settlement near Bayou LaForche).[67] This plantation, belonging to a Mr. Saint Amand, was located on the Chetimachas River, about fifty miles southeast of Pointe Coupée nearer to the Gulf of Mexico. If this was, in fact, the plantation where these absconded slaves lived, the village to which the Spanish judiciary was referring could have been any number of fugitive maroon communities between New Orleans and the Gulf of Mexico, like the maroon community near Bas du Fleuve.

Beyond these declarations of everyday resistance and intra/intergroup collaboration between enslaved and Native peoples, other significant events unfolded in Spanish Louisiana in which enslaved and free people of Afro-Native descent created rival cultural landscapes for much more radical purposes. The first was the Mina Conspiracy. In 1791 near New Roads, Louisiana, in the Pointe Coupée district, enslaved Mina people at

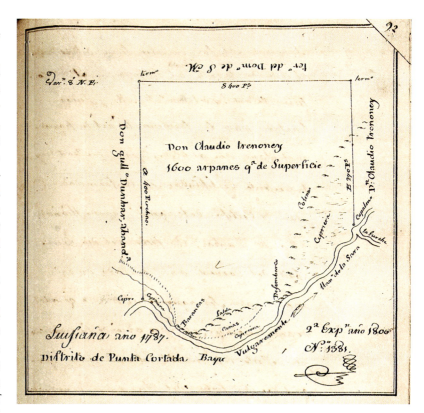

Figure 4. A 1787 survey of Claudio Trénonay's plantation in Pointe Coupée, Louisiana. Note where *la cyprière* is indicated near Bayou Sara on the center right side of the image. From the Pintado Papers, mss 890, 1223, Louisiana and Lower Mississippi Valley Collections, Louisiana State University Libraries, Baton Rouge.

several different plantations owned by a widow, Madame Provillar, devised a plan for rebellion. These enslaved people, referred to as Mina and Bambara, all spoke a certain dialect from the Mina Coast near the Bight of Benin in West Africa, and their shared language gave them a sense of comradery, according to Hall. These individuals conspired to meet at the False River to plan a revolt and kill the White residents at their respective plantations.[68]

Plantation plats from the False River indicate the intricate networks of rivers and bayous that served to connect enslaved people, including those in the Mina Conspiracy. A Mina man named Jacó, owned by a man named Pierre Fabre, was accused and imprisoned after the discovery of the Mina Conspiracy. A plantation plat of a Fabre living along the False River survives, with a "grand bayou" shown on the plat of his neighbor, a possible space where Jacó could have met neighboring enslaved people and planned this revolt (Figure 5).[69] The same illustration of plantation plats belonging to various plantations lists a Bayou du Diable (Devil's Bayou). How this bayou got its name is unclear, and the date when these plantation plats were created is not given. Perhaps the surveyor penned these plantation plats after the events unfolded in 1791, and gave the name to this bayou because of its role in the planning of the Mina Conspiracy by enslaved people. This name, Devil's Bayou, may have been a way to mark and remember this event on the landscape.[70] The cypress swamps located on these plantations offered places for enslaved people to meet and plan their revolt (see also Figure 3).

Although the Mina Conspiracy was planned a month before the slave rebellions in Saint-Domingue began, there were some similarities in the planning. Like the Mina conspirators in the cypress swamps, the slaves in Saint-Domingue planned an uprising in the woods called Bois Caïman (alligator woods). In these woods, several voodoo priests led ceremonies in which animals were sacrificed, and plans to burn down French planters' buildings were organized among priests, free people of African descent, and enslaved people. That night, August 14, 1791, the first iteration of the Haitian Revolution occurred,

which would continue until 1804.[71] It may be that the planning in the alligator woods influenced the subsequent Pointe Coupée conspirators, or perhaps the Mina conspirators who used *la cyprière* in Louisiana influenced these Haitian revolutionaries.

After the Mina Conspiracy was discovered, seventeen enslaved people were apprehended, imprisoned, and sent to New Orleans for trial. The men and women questioned feigned ignorance of the plan, and because their labor was desperately needed by their owners in Pointe Coupée, they were returned to their respective plantations. In response to the 1791 conspiracy, the governor of Louisiana, Francisco Louis Héctor, the Baron de Carondelet, passed a law that encouraged slave owners to treat their slaves more humanely. The law was based on the complaints from imprisoned Mina slaves, who described the violence, punishments, and lack of food and clothing on their plantations.[72] Governor Carondelet's compassionate response to this conspiracy enraged French planters. They accused the governor of being too lenient on enslaved people and questioned his methods in trying to make slavery in Louisiana more humane. The governor, on the other hand, believed that he had stifled a revolution by appeasing and listening to the enslaved people, and thought that his liberalization of slavery in Louisiana would keep rebellion off the minds of Louisiana's slave population.[73] These measures did not work.

The Point Coupée Rebellion and Networks of Exchange in the Atlantic World

Like the slave conspiracy in Saint-Domingue, the Pointe Coupée rebellion, organized in May 1795 by Antoine Sarrasin, involved a variety of factions including enslaved people, free people of African descent, enslaved people of Afro-Native descent, and even White Europeans from New Orleans who were politically associated with the radical revolutionary French club—the Jacobins—and influenced by extreme revolutionary thought.[74] More drastic measures were taken with the accused conspirators, since the French and Haitian Revolutions were gaining momentum and becoming more violent, and more people of European

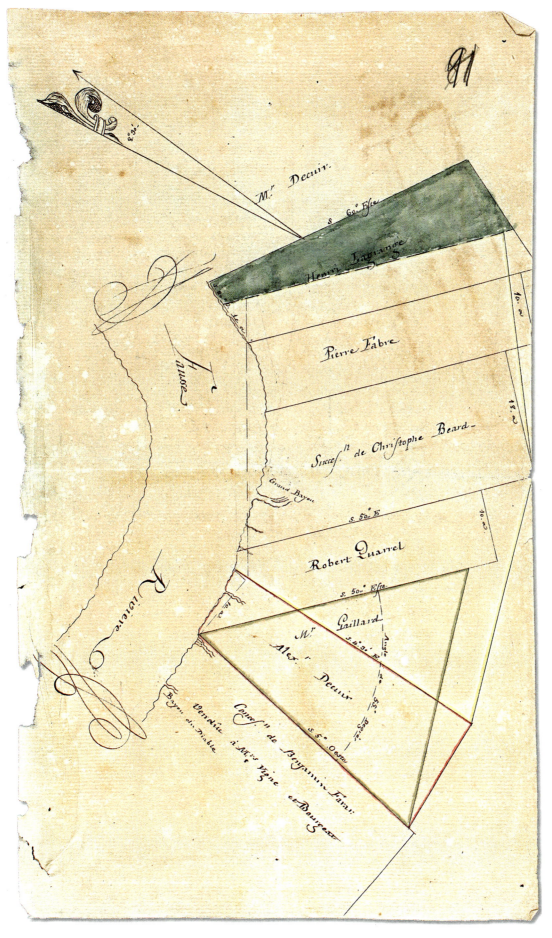

Figure 5. Plantation plat (undated) on the False River in Pointe Coupée, showing a plantation owned by Pierre Fabre, most likely the person whose enslaved man Jacó was accused of planning the 1791 Mina Conspiracy. The demarcation "Bayou du Diable" (Devil's Bayou) was possibly the surveyor's indication of enslaved people's use of this bayou to plan a rebellion. From "Plan no. [none]: Pierre Fabre; Robert Quarrel; Alexander Decuir; False River," the Pintado Papers, mss 890, 1223, Louisiana and Lower Mississippi Valley Collections, Louisiana State University Libraries, Baton Rouge.

descent were fleeing from Saint-Domingue to Louisiana to seek refuge from the increasingly bloody and radical revolution.[75] Knowledge of these Atlantic revolutions, particularly the one in Saint-Domingue, in which free people of African descent and enslaved workers took up arms to abolish plantation slavery, influenced Antoine Sarrasin and others in Louisiana.[76]

Europeans in Spanish Louisiana blamed Atlantic revolutions for this revolutionary fervor in Louisiana. Armand Allard Du Plantier, a Pointe Coupée resident and member of the French Cavalry, wrote a letter to his brother in 1795 in the aftermath of these conspiracies. He believed there was an Atlantic connection to the conspiracy, writing: "we were not calm until peace was announced. The example of St. Domingue still causes us to tremble."[77] He told his brother he regretted purchasing slaves from that island, and that he had plans to sell them if their value were to increase.[78] Du Plantier believed, therefore, that enslaved people from Saint-Domingue were to blame for bringing these revolutionary ideas to his plantations in Louisiana. What Du Plantier may not have known, or failed to recognize, was that ideas circulated quickly in the Atlantic world, and revolutionary zeal may have been spread to his Pointe Coupée plantation well before any people from Saint-Domingue arrived.

How might rebels living in Spanish Louisiana have heard about these radical currents from Saint-Domingue and other spaces in the Atlantic world? Julius Scott has argued that enslaved and free people of African descent who worked on boats spread this revolutionary fervor via their commercial trade routes throughout the Atlantic basin. By traveling from one port city to the next and talking to people from disparate parts of the Atlantic, mariners spread news and gossip which connected Europe with the Caribbean, the Caribbean with Spanish Louisiana, and port cities with plantations.[79] What fostered these transmissions of knowledge, Scott argues, in addition to these commercial networks, was the oral tradition among Afro-Americans. He argued that unlike European traditions of spreading news through print, Afro-Americans in the Caribbean transmitted news, rumors, and information ver-

bally.[80] These "scraps of news, conflicting interpretations, elusive facts, and shifting rumors" spread through port cities via enslaved and free people of African descent along with the goods that went from the ports to the hinterlands and plantations, contributing to the creation of rival cultural landscapes.[81]

Boatmen spread their knowledge and gossip from one port city to the next, from French Saint-Domingue to British Kingston, from Dutch Curaçao to Spanish New Orleans. Enslaved people from plantations came to these port cities to load and unload cargo, and discussed political and social currents with these boatmen from disparate parts of the Caribbean; runaway slaves found work in these large Atlantic cities, and spread gossip and rumors from one runaway to the next, who might go back to the plantation and spread this news. Scott found that information traveled quickly in the Atlantic world via commercial trading routes, especially among people of African descent, so it should come as no surprise that enslaved people in Pointe Coupée were highly aware of and invested in the rumors of rebellion and revolution stemming from Saint-Domingue.

Antoine Sarrasin tapped into these communication networks swirling around the Atlantic basin through his access to the False and Mississippi Rivers through his work loading and unloading indigo, sugar, and other commodities on boats. As previously noted, he testified that he heard that the king of Spain had freed the slaves in Louisiana from freedmen of African descent traveling from New Orleans to Natchez.[82] Sarrasin's experience of hearing rumors regarding slavery and emancipation was not an isolated event: enslaved people in Martinique believed slavery had been abolished in 1789 during the French Revolution, since at the same time members of the Estates-General in France were discussing gradual emancipation.[83] Similarly, enslaved people in Guadeloupe believed slavery had ended for them because French revolutionaries had "dethroned their king" in 1790.[84] These events, among others that Sarrasin experienced in Pointe Coupée, highlight the historical support of royalism among some groups of enslaved people and people of African descent in the Atlantic world, and these rumors regarding slavery, abolition, and emancipation connected marginalized groups of people and revolutionaries across the Atlantic, even in remote places like Pointe Coupée.[85]

Antoine Sarrasin did not act alone in planning a violent, well-organized overthrow of White mastery in Pointe Coupée in 1795. Close to seventy people were accused in the plot, and because the Spanish government allowed enslaved people to testify and state their case, court records of their individual versions of the story survive. The conspirators and those accused of being involved stated their plan was to set fire to plantation buildings, seize weapons, and kill all Whites within the Pointe Coupée district. Most of the enslaved people accused of planning this revolt lived at plantations belonging to Julien Poydras. Sixty-three people were arrested and imprisoned in New Orleans. Twenty-three men were executed, including Antoine Sarrasin. Unlike the Mina Conspiracy, the Pointe Coupée rebellion involved a diverse group of planners. One of them, a European tutor named Joseph Bouyavel, admitted to discussing the French Revolution's radical goals with enslaved and free people of African descent on Pedro Goudeau's plantation, where he was employed.[86]

According to the testimonies of those accused of being part of the rebellion, the planners relied upon the swamps of these plantations to plan their attack, and *la cyprière* was mentioned quite often in these court testimonies as a specific place where everyone knew to meet to plan this revolution. The use of the cypress swamps by Sarrasin and others indicated that these spaces were believed to be inaccessible to the White population. The use of the cypress swamps also indicates that enslaved people like Sarrasin knew how to navigate these swamps and which ones were more secretive and better to meet in than other spaces, away from the White gaze. Whereas some historians characterize the environment of the Lower Mississippi River Valley as carceral because of its inhospitable features, including swamps, these spaces were actually helpful and central for establishing communication networks among enslaved people at Pointe Coupée.[87] When Ami, an enslaved woman belonging to the Widow Barron, testified about her knowledge of the rebellion in 1795, she declared that most of the planning unfolded in the swamps, including the election of Antoine Sarrasin to serve as their leader.[88]

The conspirators who testified about their involvement mentioned *la cyprière* as a central space of planning this revolt, thereby demonstrating that enslaved people like Sarrasin used the swamps to create an oppositional geography to White geographic domination.[89] Thimothée, who belonged to Widow Lacour, testified that other slaves from the Lacour plantation met in the cypress swamp to organize supplying arms and ammunition.[90] Louis, a slave belonging to Pedro Goudeau, stated in his declaration that all of the plans were made in the cypress swamp.[91] Jacob, who also belonged to Widow Lacour, testified that these enslaved people had met in *la cyprière* to discuss these plans, though he was not part of the conspiracy; he was simply in the same cypress swamp when he overheard them.[92] Jacob's testimony, in which he claims innocence of the crime of conspiring, demonstrates the quotidian aspect of enslaved people simply being in the swamps, which did not raise suspicion in the court.

Joseph Mina (of no relation to the Mina Conspiracy) said in his testimony that part of the plan included hiding out in the cypress swamps until the leaders gave the word to strike.[93] Antoine Sarrasin held secret meetings in his cabin to plan the revolt. We do not know on which particular Poydras plantation Sarrasin lived when planning this revolt, but some of Poydras's plantation plats still exist.[94] One extant plantation survey depicts a plantation along Bayou Sara, which flowed into the Mississippi River.[95] It might be in these cypress swamps on Bayou Sara that Antoine Sarrasin planned the rebellion. Another plantation plat places one of Poydras's plantations along the Mississippi River and near the plantations owned by others whose bondsmen and women were involved in this conspiracy, which illustrates the spatial communication networks within the plantation network, and how Sarrasin was able to choose a space centralized and accessible for neighboring enslaved individuals.[96]

These plantation plats give us a glimpse into

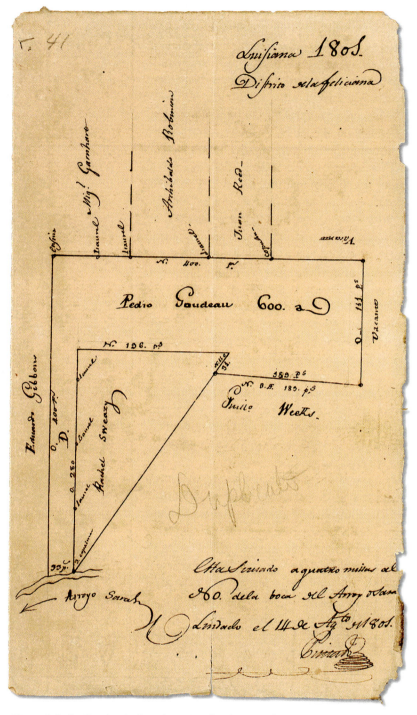

Figure 6. Pedro Goudeau's 1801 plantation plat along Bayou Sara ("Arroyo Sara") at the bottom left-hand corner. Courtesy of the Pintado Papers, mss 890, 1223, Louisiana and Lower Mississippi Valley Collections, Louisiana State University Libraries, Baton Rouge.

the intimate Black spaces where enslaved and free people of African and Native descent met to plan a conspiracy and create a rival cultural landscape. Pedro Goudeau's estate backed up to "Arroyo Sara," probably indicating Bayou Sara, like one of the plantations of Julien Poydras (Figure 6).[97] The estate of Martin Bourgeat, where several enslaved people were tried for the rebellion, was located along the False River, and his nearby neighbor was Julien Poydras (Figure 7). Sarrasin had called for a meeting in the slave quarters of Widow Bourgeat, since there were ample spaces for them to meet on this plantation, including some bayous, cypress swamps, and paths near the False River.[98]

The stories of two Native women, Françoise and Madelaine, demonstrate the role Native people played in the Pointe Coupée rebellion from their close proximity to the cypress swamps. Although their stories are more difficult to decipher, it is clear from their testimony that they were both in the cypress swamp with enslaved workers on the Lacour plantation. Françoise and Madelaine were Tunica Indians who lived on the plantation of Widow Lacour and presumably worked for her as free laborers. All we know about these two women comes from their brief statements to the court, in which they both claim they were in the swamp. According to them, they were caught in a storm in a cypress swamp, where they overheard enslaved workers discussing their goal to move the "event" from Saturday to Sunday.[99] The testimonies of Françoise and Madelaine fail to mention whether they themselves alerted the White members at the Lacour plantation about this rebellion, but others who testified claim the Tunica women were responsible for telling the Whites and thwarting the rebellion.[100] When asked, both Françoise and Madelaine claimed that after hearing these allegations leveled by the slave community, they were scared to leave their cabins.[101] This detail is important, since it tells us that these women felt threatened by the revolutionary fervor found in the swamps. Although we do not know whether the Tunica women on the Lacour plantation had conspired with Antoine Sarrasin and others, they were present in the swamps when the conspirators were planning. By later distancing themselves from this space—*la cyprière*—which was now used as a planning zone for rebellion, we can infer that these Native women were aware of the power associated with being in these swamps, now transformed into a space of Black liberation.

Conclusion

Antoine Sarrasin and the others endeavored to make the swamps within the plantation networks in Point Coupée an invisible space of Black liberation, but the Spanish saw them and recognized their revolutionary efforts. The official Spanish response—the trial and subsequent execution of the accused—further transformed these same swamps into a space of political and social oppression. After the twenty-three accused, including Antoine Sarrasin, were hanged, the leaders' heads were severed from their bodies and placed on pikes along the False River on the plantation where Sarrasin and others were enslaved.[102] Other severed heads were placed on pikes running from Pointe Coupée to New Orleans following the course of the Mississippi.[103]

The decision to place the severed heads on pikes along the same spaces where the rebellions were organized was a physical, visceral political statement that directly responded to Sarrasin's use of the swamps to organize a rebellion.[104] The Spanish responded to Sarrasin's creation of a rival cultural landscape, recognized it, and reasserted their claims and authority over it. Just as Antoine Sarrasin and other enslaved people used portions of the plantation landscape to create a rival cultural landscape, the Spanish manipulated the same landscape to make a political statement to discourage others from following suit. In the same way that the Spanish militia invaded the maroon community near the mouth of the Mississippi, Bas du Fleuve, in 1784, the Spanish invaded (though without an army) the spaces that Sarrasin and others had carefully created and cultivated to fit their particular needs in planning this rebellion. The same paths along the False and Mississippi Rivers that Sarrasin walked, where he heard rumors of the king of

Figure 7. Estate of Martin Bourgeat, with neighbor Julien Poydras, along the "Rio Fausse" (bottom right-hand corner). Notice the many bayous and *la cyprière* depicted on Poydras's estate, perhaps where Antoine Sarrasin held meetings with neighboring enslaved people. Plan no. [none]: Alexander Decuire; Martin Bourgeat; Joseph Aguiar; 1803. Courtesy of the Pintado Papers, mss 890, 1223, Louisiana and Lower Mississippi Valley Collections, Louisiana State University Libraries, Baton Rouge.

Spain freeing slaves, where he thought about his legal case as an Afro-Native man, and where he heard that the Afro-Creoles, just like himself, were gaining momentum in Saint-Domingue, became his final resting place—though his dismembered body undermined the eternal peace we expect in death.

In spite of the failure of Sarrasin's rebellion, Spanish colonial officials and subsequent American officials could never successfully keep enslaved and free people of African descent from exploiting certain parts of the plantation landscape and creating rival cultural landscapes, not only in Louisiana but in the wider Atlantic world.[105] Through their court testimony, those involved confirmed Sarrasin's precision in planning the rebellion and the cunning choice of the physical space to enact it. Sarrasin *made* the cypress swamps revolutionary spaces. His intimate knowledge of *la cyprière* reveals the familiarity with and mastery of the natural world that many enslaved and free people of African descent possessed during the eighteenth and nineteenth centuries. Historians and geographers are beginning to map Black geographic experiences throughout the African diaspora and recover routes and paths that enslaved and free people of African descent "invisibly" marked on the landscape to contest White geographic domination.[106]

Sarrasin's story illustrates the creation of a particular Black geographic experience in the diaspora. Though his rebellion and others may have failed, Sarrasin was a revolutionary hero. He knew not only how to organize a diverse group of people, but also how to spread revolutionary Atlantic ideas throughout his world. His idea of immediate freedom from slavery was radical in the world in which he lived. Sarrasin's efforts—and his willingness to die for his cause—inspired others to keep challenging the parameters of slavery until abolition was made a reality in the nineteenth century. Though many others no doubt acted similarly, their stories have been lost in the modern archive. Finding ways to creatively and critically engage with the past to recover the stories of those like Sarrasin, such as using the landscape as a category of historical analysis, is one way we can create better history, and give historical figures like Sarrasin the respect he was not given in his lifetime, and deserves in ours.

AUTHOR BIOGRAPHY

Tessa Evans completed her doctorate in early American history at the University of Tennessee in 2020. Her research uses interdisciplinary methods to examine how diverse groups of people—including Native Americans, Europeans, and people of African descent—created radical counter-geographies in small, highly disputed locations in the Lower Mississippi River Valley.

ACKNOWLEDGMENTS

I would like to thank Kristen Block, Julie Reed, Robert Bland, Barbara Heath, and Bob Hutton for their valuable comments and support during the writing of this article. I would also like to thank the anonymous reviewers as well as editors Michael Chiarappa and Margaret Grubiak for their generous feedback and suggestions.

NOTES

1. Declaration of Antoine Sarrasin, May 11, 1795, Louisiana Slave Conspiracies, http://lsc.berkeley.edu. The original documents from the Pointe Coupée conspiracy are located in the Pointe Coupée Parish Courthouse in New Roads, Louisiana. A website has recently been created at the University of California, Berkeley, called Louisiana Slave Conspiracies, in which a team of historians, translators, and web designers have uploaded images, transcriptions, and translations of the original documents regarding both the Mina Conspiracy and Pointe Coupée rebellion. See https://lsc.berkeley.edu/ for the website and its information. All citations from the Mina and Pointe Coupée conspiracies are from Louisiana Slave Conspiracies unless otherwise noted.

2. Monique Allewaert, *Ariel's Ecology: Plantations, Personhood, and Colonialism in the American Tropics* (Minneapolis: University of Minnesota Press, 2013), 47.

3. The birth year of Antoine Sarrasin is approximate, but he claimed in his court testimony he was thirty-eight years old at the time of his arrest, making his birth year 1757. Gwendolyn Midlo Hall, *Africans in Colonial Louisiana: The Development of Afro-Creole Culture in the Eighteenth Century* (Baton Rouge: Louisiana State University Press, 1992), 243. See also Jack D. Holmes, "The Abortive Slave Revolt at Pointe Coupée, Louisiana, 1795," *Louisiana History: The Journal of the Louisiana Historical Association* 11, no. 4 (1970): 341–62; and Gilbert C. Din, "Carondelet, the Cabildo, and Slaves: Louisiana in 1795," *Louisiana History: The Journal of the Louisiana Historical Association* 38, no. 1 (1997): 5–28.

4. Katherine McKittrick utilizes the term "geographic materialities" in her work *Demonic Grounds: Black Women and the Cartographies of Struggle* (Minneapolis: University of Minnesota Press, 2006), xx.

5. McKittrick, *Demonic Grounds*; Stephanie Camp, *Closer to Freedom: Enslaved Women and Everyday Resistance in the Plantation South* (Chapel Hill: University of North Carolina Press, 2004); and Rashauna Johnson, *Slavery's Metropolis: Unfree Labor in New Orleans during the Age of Revolutions* (Cambridge: Cambridge University Press, 2016).

6. Allewaert, *Ariel's Ecology*; Jessica Bridget George, "'A New and More Vigorous Growth': Resilience and Southern Ecologies in Antebellum Literature," *ISLE: Interdisciplinary Studies in Literature and*

Environment (2022): isaco34, https://doi.org/10.1093/isle/isaco34.

7. For colonial extensions of control and the creation of political landscapes, see Steve Kosiba and Andrew M. Bauer, "Mapping the Political Landscape: Toward a GIS Analysis of Environmental and Social Difference," *Journal of Archaeological Method and Theory* 20 (2013): 61–101; and Angèle Smith, "Mapped Landscapes: The Politics of Metaphor, Knowledge, and Representation on Nineteenth-Century Irish Ordnance Survey Maps," *Historical Archaeology* 44, no. 1 (2007): 81–91. For plantation landscapes curtailing social mobility, see Dell Upton, "White and Black Landscapes in Eighteenth-Century Virginia," *Places Journal* 2, no. 2 (1984): 59–72.

8. Kosiba and Bauer, "Mapping the Political Landscape."

9. See Suzanne M. Spencer-Wood, "A Feminist Framework for Analyzing Powered Cultural Landscapes in Historical Archaeology," *International Journal of Historical Archaeology* 14, no. 4 (2010): 518.

10. Hall, *Africans in Colonial Louisiana*, 243. For the most recent work on these Native bands and tribes during the age of European exploration, see Elizabeth Ellis, *The Great Power of Small Nations: Indigenous Diplomacy in the Gulf South* (Philadelphia: University of Pennsylvania Press, 2022).

11. For more on borderlands in the Native South, see Alejandra Dubcovsky, *Informed Power: Communication in the Early American South* (Cambridge, Mass.: Harvard University Press, 2016); Kathleen DuVal, *The Native Ground: Indians and Colonists in the Heart of the Continent* (Philadelphia: University of Pennsylvania Press, 2006); and Andrew K. Frank and Glenn Crothers, eds., *Borderland Narratives: Negotiation and Accommodation in North America's Contested Spaces, 1500–1850* (Gainesville: University Press of Florida, 2017).

12. Hall, *Africans in Colonial Louisiana*, 262.

13. Hall, *Africans in Colonial Louisiana*, 262.

14. For example, "Succession of Sr. Nicolas Sarrazin" from the French Superior Council (April 25, 1758) states, "Sieur François Sarrasin, resident of Arkansas, grants a procuration to Sieur Antoine Sarrazin, his brother, resident of Pointe Coupée, giving him power and authority to recover his share of their mother's [Dame François Rolland], deceased wife of Sieur Jean Stephane, estates, movables, and immovables." Document 7444, "Spanish Colonial Document Index Bind-ers: 1769–1804," Colonial Documents, Louisiana State Museum Special Collections, New Orleans.

15. There are many different spellings of the surname "Sarassin" from both primary sources and secondary sources. I rely upon the spelling of the surname based on the primary source, which, in this case, has Nicholas's last named spelled "Sarrazin."

16. Ann Dubuisson, "François Sarazin: Interpreter at Arkansas Post during the Chickasaw Wars," *Arkansas Historical Quarterly* 71, no. 3 (2012): 243.

17. Historians write that no documentary evidence exists that lists François as the father of Saracen, but as Ann Dubuisson writes, most children born of French-Quapaw unions were named after their father. Furthermore, "there was probably no disapproval on either side of a young Quapaw woman having a child by a young French cadet," she writes, since François most likely fathered this child before his marriage to Marie Leipin. Dubuisson, "François Sarazin," 260.

18. "Saracen," the Quapaw Nation, https://www.quapawtribe.com/598/Saracen. It is also of interest to note that the new Quapaw Casino in Pine Bluff, Arkansas, the ancestral homelands of the Quapaw people, is named Saracen Casino.

19. "Receipt and Discharge," French Superior Council, June 4, 1748, Document 30949, "Colonial Documents Black Books Reference Page," Louisiana State Museum Special Collections, New Orleans, https://www.crt.state.la.us/louisiana-state-museum/collections/historical-center/colonial-documents/index.

20. "Act of Exchange," Spanish Judicial, February 6, 1762, Document 8085, "Spanish Colonial Document Index Binders: 1769–1804," Colonial Documents, Louisiana State Museum Special Collections, New Orleans.

21. "Bonnaventure Succession," Spanish Judicial, May 11, 1762, Document 8165, "Spanish Colonial Document Index Binders: 1769–1804," Colonial Documents, Louisiana State Museum Special Collections, New Orleans.

22. Hall, *Africans in Colonial Louisiana*, 340.

23. "Sale of a Negress," French Superior Council, September 28, 1744, listed in *Louisiana Historical Quarterly* 13, no. 1 (1930): 158.

24. "Power of Attorney," Spanish Judicial, June 6, 1766, Document 80821, "Spanish Colonial Document Index Binders: 1769–1804," Colonial Documents, Louisiana State Museum Special Collections, New Orleans.

25. Hall, *Africans in Colonial Louisiana*, 341.

26. Hall, *Africans in Colonial Louisiana*, 340.

27. Hall, *Africans in Colonial Louisiana*, 336. Spanish governor Alejandro O'Reilly issued a formal decree on December 7, 1769, that outlawed enslavement of Natives of any kind in the Louisiana colony, and the subsequent Spanish governor Esteban Rodriguez Miro republished O'Reilly's ordinance in 1787. Many historians have written on Native slavery and its rise and eventual demise in North America. See Leila K. Blackbird, "A Gendered Frontier: Métissage and Indigenous Enslavement in Eighteenth-Century Basse-Louisiane," *Eighteenth-Century Studies* 56, no. 2 (2023): 205–12; Christina Snyder, *Slavery in Indian Country: The Changing Face of Captivity in Early America* (Cambridge, Mass.: Harvard University Press, 2012); and Alan Gallay, *The Indian Slave Trade: The Rise of the English Empire in the American South, 1670–1717* (New Haven, Conn.: Yale University Press, 2003), for analysis of how the Native slave trade functioned in various spaces in North America. Stephen Webre writes about Indian slavery in Spanish Louisiana specifically. See Stephen Webre, "The Problem of Indian Slavery in Spanish Louisiana, 1793–1803," *Louisiana History: The Journal of the Louisiana Historical Association* 25, no. 2 (1984): 117–35.

28. "Affidavit," French Superior Records, Document Number 4, listed in *Louisiana Historical Quarterly* 5, no. 3 (1922): 426.

29. "Declaration: Despalliere and des Roussels," Spanish Judicial, May 9, 1767, Document 2144, "Spanish Colonial Document Index Binders: 1769–1804," Colonial Documents, Louisiana State Museum Collections, New Orleans.

30. Daniel Usner details the connections forged between enslaved and free people of African descent and Native Americans in the Lower Mississippi River Valley. See Daniel Usner, *Indians, Settlers, and Slaves in a Frontier Exchange Economy: The Lower Mississippi Valley Before 1783* (Chapel Hill: University of North Carolina Press, 1992).

31. All of the legal cases surrounding the trial of Antoine Sarrasin list him as a mulatto, but in his "Confession," Sarrasin refers to himself as a Creole. "Confession of Antoine Sarrassin of Sr. Poedras," May 16, 1795, found under "Documents," Louisiana Slave Conspiracies, https://lsc.berkeley.edu.

32. *Manuel Bourguignon v. Succession of Dame Louis Perthuis*, Spanish Judicial, 1791, Document 2684, file 1500, box 62, "Spanish Colonial Document Index Binders: 1769–1804," Colonial Documents, Louisiana State Museum Collections, New Orleans.

33. *Manuel Bourguignon v. Succession of Dame Louis Perthuis*, Spanish Judicial, 1791, Document 2684, file 1500, box 62, "Spanish Colonial Document Index Binders: 1769–1804," Colonial Documents, Louisiana State Museum Collections, New Orleans.

34. Hall, *Africans in Colonial Louisiana*, 239, 259.

35. "Contract between Pierre Ricard and François Allain with a Free Mulatto Named Louis," Spanish Judicial, October 9, 1762, Document 8284, "Spanish Colonial Document Index Binders: 1769–1804," Colonial Documents, Louisiana State Museum Collections, New Orleans.

36. Hall, *Africans in Colonial Louisiana*, 340.

37. Hall, *Africans in Colonial Louisiana*, 341.

38. Historians have discussed the historical relationship between enslaved people and the shifting geopolitical landscapes, and in particular how enslaved and free people of African descent navigated these legal landscapes in the changing Atlantic world for their own benefit. For some of the most recent work, see Ariela Gross and Alejandro de la Fuente, *Becoming Free, Becoming Black: Race, Freedom, and Law in Cuba, Virginia, and Louisiana* (Cambridge, Mass.: Harvard University Press, 2020); Brian Owensby and Richard Ross, eds., *Justice in a New World: Negotiating Legal Intelligibility in British, Iberian, and Indigenous America* (New York: New York University Press, 2018); and Nancy O. Gallman, "Reconstituting Power in an American Borderland: Political Change in Colonial East Florida," *Florida Historical Quarterly* 94, no. 2 (2015): 169–91.

39. "Declaration of Ami (Widow Barron)," May 10, 1795, Louisiana Slave Conspiracies, https://lsc.berkeley.edu/.

40. Kurt Anschuetz, Richard H. Wilshusen, and Cherie L. Scheick, "An Archaeology of Landscapes: Perspectives and Directions," *Journal of Archaeological Research* 9, no. 2 (2001): 161; and John J. Winberry, "The Geographic Concept of Landscape: The History of a Paradigm," in *Carolina's Historical Landscapes*, ed. Linda F. Stine, Martha Zierden, Lesley M. Drucker, and Christopher Judge (Knoxville: University of Tennessee Press, 1997), 1–14.

41. Upton, "White and Black Landscapes," 1; Suzanne M. Spencer-Wood, "A Feminist Framework for Analyzing Powered Cultural Landscapes in Historical Archaeology," *International Journal of Historical Archaeology* 14, no. 4 (2010): 507. For the watercolor paintings of Father Paret, see Marcel Boyer and Jay D. Edwards, eds., *Plantations by the River: Watercolor Paintings from St. Charles Parish, Louisiana, by Father Joseph M. Paret, 1859* (Baton Rouge: Geoscience Publications, Department of Geography and Anthropology, Louisiana State University, 2002).

42. John Michael Vlach, *Back of the Big House: The Architecture of Plantation Slavery* (Chapel Hill: University of North Carolina Press, 1993).

43. Upton, "White and Black Landscapes," 1

44. Anschuetz et al., "An Archaeology of Landscapes," 161.

45. Spencer-Wood, "A Feminist Framework for Analyzing Powered Cultural Landscapes," 518.

46. Camp, *Closer to Freedom*, 7.

47. Johnson, *Slavery's Metropolis*, 71.

48. Allewaert, *Ariel's Ecology*, 33–41.

49. Allewaert, *Ariel's Ecology*, 33. This argument about swamps as "Africanized spaces" builds on the work of Gwendolyn Midlo Hall, who stated that Louisiana was more African than European in her work *Africans in Colonial Louisiana,* and this argument was one of her most important historiographical interventions.

50. Peirce F. Lewis discusses the creation and characteristics of backswamps in *New Orleans: The Making of an Urban Landscape* (Cambridge, Mass.: Ballinger Publishing, 1976), 22–23. Backswamps are the low-lying area behind a river's natural levee that often flood.

51. Lewis, *New Orleans*, 22–23.

52. See Joseph DeCuir's 1802 Plantation Plat at Pointe Coupée, Pintado Papers, Mss. 890, 1223, Louisiana and Lower Mississippi Valley Collections, Louisiana State University Libraries, Baton Rouge.

53. Hall, *Africans in Colonial Louisiana*, 205.

54. These plats are available in the Pintado Papers, Louisiana State University Special Collections, Baton Rouge, and the Louisiana Digital Library, https://louisianadigitallibrary.org/islandora/object/lsu-sc-pintado:collection. Search "Pointe Coupée" for images of these particular plats or by the surnames "Lamar," "Alston," and "Richet."

55. Allewaert, *Ariel's Ecology*, 33.

56. Allewaert, *Ariel's Ecology*, 33.

57. For more on maroon communities in the Atlantic world, see Chapter 1 in Allewaert, *Ariel's Ecology*; Richard Price, *Alibi's World* (Baltimore: Johns Hopkins University Press, 1990); Kenneth Bilby, *True Born Maroons* (Gainesville: University Press of Florida, 2005); Gabino La Rosa Corzo, *Runaway Slave Settlements in Cuba: Resistance and Repression* (Chapel Hill: University of North Carolina Press, 2003); Vincent Brown, *Tacky's Revolt: The Story of an Atlantic Slave War* (Cambridge, Mass.: Harvard University Press, 2020); Richard Bodek and Joseph Kelly, eds., *Maroons and the Marooned: Runaways and Castaways in the Americas* (Jackson: University of Mississippi Press, 2020); and Jane Landers, *Black Society in Spanish Florida* (Champaign: University of Illinois Press, 1999).

58. Hall, chapter 7, "Bas du Fleuve: The Creole Slaves Adapt to the Cypress Swamp," *Africans in Colonial Louisiana*, 201–36.

59. Hall, *Africans in Colonial Louisiana*, 253.

60. "Examination of Runaway Geula," French Superior Council Record, January 10, 1737, No. 37, repr. in *Louisiana Historical Quarterly* 5, no. 3 (1922–23): 386.

61. "Interrogation of Francois, slave of M. Bousclair," *Records of the Superior Council of Louisiana* 19, no. 3 (1936): 769–71. For the original in French, see "Suit against Francois, negro slave of Mr. Boisclaire and accomplice," May 18, 1748, Document No. 48/84, "Louisiana Colonial Documents," Louisiana Historical Center, New Orleans, http://www.lacolonialdocs.org/document/8042.

62. "Examination of Bizago, Negro," Spanish Judicial Records, February 21, 1767, Document 2041, "Spanish Colonial Document Index Binders: 1769–1804," Colonial Documents, Louisiana State Museum Collections, New Orleans.

63. "Interrogatory of Bizago, Negro," Spanish Judicial Records, March 12, 1767, Document 67, "Spanish Colonial Document Index Binders: 1769–1804," Colonial Documents, Louisiana State Museum Collections, New Orleans.

64. "Confrontation of Bizago," Spanish Judicial Records, March 12, 1767, Document 2058, "Spanish Colonial Document Index Binders: 1769–1804," Colonial Documents, Louisiana State Museum Collections, New Orleans.

65. "Examination of Bizago, Negro," Spanish Judicial Records, March 14, 1767, Document 2065, "Spanish Colonial Document Index Binders: 1769–1804," Colonial Documents, Louisiana State Museum Collections, New Orleans.

66. "Motion to Try Runaway Indian Slave," French Superior Council, April 9, 1727, repr. in *Louisiana Historical Quarterly* 3, no. 3 (1920): 444.

67. "Plan No. 1485: Alexandre Daspie de Saint Amant, Valanzuela, 1801," Pintado Papers, Louisiana State University Special Collections, Baton Rouge, and in Louisiana Digital Library, https://louisianadigital library.org/islandora/object/lsu-sc-pintado%3A663.

68. Hall, *Africans in Colonial Louisiana*, 320–21. See "Declaration of Jaco (Fabre)," July 11, 1791, Louisiana Slave Conspiracies, https://lsc.berkeley.edu/, where he mentions meeting people at the False River.

69. "Plan no. [none]: Pierre Fabre; Robert Quarrel; Alexander Decuir; False River," Pintado Papers, Louisiana State University Special Collections, Baton Rouge, https://louisianadigitallibrary.org/islandora/object/lsu-sc-pintado%3A1412.

70. The surveyor, Vicente Pintado, was hired by Governor Carondelet to survey and plat lands held by individuals in Spanish Louisiana from the 1790s to 1803.

71. See Laurent Dubois, *Avengers of the New World: The Story of the Haitian Revolution* (Cambridge, Mass.: Harvard University Press, 2005), 100–103.

72. Ulysses S. Ricard, "The Pointe Coupée Slave Conspiracy of 1791," *Proceedings of the Meeting of the French Colonial Historical Society* 15 (1992): 127.

73. Royal Decree of October 21, 1798, Council of the Indies, AGI, Audiencia de Santo Domingo, leg. 2531. "Those settlers ought to realize that Negroes are men and under the protection of the laws, that their masters can correct in a paternal fashion their excesses and indolence and denounce their crimes to the Superior Government so that they may be investigated and proven in due form, and that may be punished following that formality which is hereby commanded." As quoted in Holmes, "The Abortive Slave Revolt at Pointe Coupée," 344.

74. Wim Klooster, "The French Revolution," in *Revolutions in the Atlantic World: A Comparative History* (New York: New York University Press, 2009), 65–67. For more specific information on Jacobinism in New Orleans and Louisiana, see Hall, chapter 10,

"Unrest During the Early 1790s," *Africans in Colonial Louisiana*, 317–20.

75. Holmes, "The Abortive Slave Revolt at Pointe Coupée," 344.

76. Wim Klooster, "From Prize Colony to Black Independence: The Revolution in Haiti," in *Revolutions in the Atlantic World*, 84–116.

77. Armand Allard DuPlantier, letter to his brother, Guy Allard Duplantier, January 10, 1795, Armand DuPlantier Family Papers, Louisiana State University Special Collections, Baton Rouge, and Louisiana Digital Library (*Cela nous n'étions pas tranquille jusqu'au moment où Lon nous à publie La Paix, l'exemple de St. Domingue nous fait encore trembler, j'ai bien du regret d'en avoir acheté un nombre, s'il reprenoit un peu de valeur, je ne tarderois pas à men défaire*).

78. Armand Allard DuPlantier, letter to his brother, Guy Allard Duplantier, January 10, 1795.

79. Julius S. Scott, *The Common Wind: Afro-American Currents in the Age of the Haitian Revolution* (London: Verso Press, 2018).

80. Scott, *The Common Wind*, 77.

81. Scott, *The Common Wind*, 77.

82. "Declaration of Antoine Sarrasin, Poydras," May 11, 1795, Louisiana Slave Conspiracies, https://lsc.berkeley.edu.

83. Klooster, *Revolutions in the Atlantic World*, 98.

84. Klooster, *Revolutions in the Atlantic World*, 98.

85. For a brief overview of the historiography of popular royalism among diverse groups of people in the Atlantic world, see Marcelle Echeverri, "Presentation: Monarchy, Empire, and Popular Politics in the Atlantic Age of Revolutions," *Varia Historia* 35, no. 67 (January/April 2019): 15–35.

86. "Testimony of Joseph Bouyavel," May 18, 1795, Louisiana Slave Conspiracies, https://lsc.berkeley. edu. Gwendolyn Hall most famously contends that the Pointe Coupée conspiracy was a manifestation of the French and Haitian Jacobin spirits in Louisiana, claiming that "A copy of the Declaration of the Rights of Man" was found in the cabin of certain enslaved people in Pointe Coupée, but she cites no evidence or footnotes to corroborate this claim. See Gwendolyn Hall, "The 1795 Slave Conspiracy in Pointe Coupée: Impact of the French Revolution," *Proceedings of the Meeting of the French Colonial Historical Society* 15 (1992): 130–41, 37.

87. Walter Johnson claims the Lower Mississippi

River Valley was a carceral landscape for those enslaved in chapter 8, "The Carceral Landscape." *River of Dark Dreams: Slavery and Empire in the Cotton Kingdom* (Cambridge, Mass.: Harvard University Press, 2013). For an examination of how enslaved people utilized these "marginalized" swamplands in antebellum and postbellum Arkansas and Louisiana, see Tessa Evans, "From Swamps to Swamping: The Usage and Perceptions of Swamps by African-Americans in Antebellum and Postbellum Arkansas and Louisiana" (master's thesis, James Madison University, 2014), 196.

88. "Declaration of Ami, Widow Barron," May 10, 1795, Louisiana Slave Conspiracies, https://lsc.berkeley.edu/ (*Il devait s'en informer que quelques jours avait lui déclarant était à la cyprière arriverent son frère François et Jean Louis esclave à la Veuve Barron, envoyé par le camp à Mr Poedras [sic] pour lui proposer de la faire chef de la révolution*).

89. McKittrick, *Demonic Grounds*, 6.

90. "Declaration of Thimothée, Widow Lacour," May 14, 1795, Louisiana Slave Conspiracies, https://lsc.berkeley.edu/.

91. "Declaration of Louis, Goudeau," May 8, 1795, Louisiana Slave Conspiracies, https://lsc.berkeley.edu/.

92. "Declaration of Jacob, Widow Lacour," May 13, 1795, Louisiana Slave Conspiracies, https://lsc.berkeley.edu/.

93. "Declaration of Joseph Mina," May 9, 1795, Louisiana Slave Conspiracies, https://lsc.berkeley.edu/.

94. Hall, *Africans in Colonial Louisiana*, 362.

95. "Juan Beauvais; Julien Poydras; Carlos Beauvais; Armando Duplantier; Huberto Powel," Plantation Plats, no date, Pintado Papers, Louisiana State University Special Collections, Baton Rouge, and Louisiana Digital Library, https://louisianadigitallibrary.org/islandora/search/Poydras?type=edismax&cp=lsu-sc-pintado%3Acollection.

96. See Poydras Estate under "Places," Louisiana Slave Conspiracies, https://lsc.berkeley.edu/places.

97. Plan no. [none]: Pedro Goudeau; Feliciana, 1801, Pintado Papers, Louisiana State University Spe-

cial Collections, Baton Rouge, and Louisiana Digital Library, https://louisianadigitallibrary.org/islandora/object/lsu-sc-pintado%3A1249.

98. Antoine Sarrasin mentions in his Declaration that they met at one point on the bridge at False River (*l'affaire de l'assemblée au pont du chemin de la fausse rivière*). "Declaration of Antoine Sarrassin," May 11, 1795, Louisiana Slave Conspiracies, https://lsc.berkeley.edu/.

99. "Declaration of Madelaine," April 27, 1795, Louisiana Slave Conspiracies, https://lsc.berkeley.edu/.

100. "Confrontation of Marcos Lich and his crew with Jeanne and others," May 15, 1795, Louisiana Slave Conspiracies, https://lsc.berkeley.edu/.

101. "Statement of Françoise," May 6, 1795, Louisiana Slave Conspiracies, https://lsc.berkeley.edu/.

102. "Execution of the Sentence of Point Coupée Conspiracy," May 29, 1795, Louisiana Slave Conspiracies, https://lsc.berkeley.edu/.

103. Holmes, "The Abortive Slave Revolt at Pointe Coupée," 352–53.

104. Vincent Brown, "Spiritual Terror and Sacred Authority in Jamaica," *Slavery and Abolition* 24, no. 1 (2003): 24–53.

105. In addition to the writings of Stephanie Camp and Katherine McKittrick, there is a growing historiography regarding space and slavery in the United States and Atlantic world. See Anthony Kaye, *Joining Places: Slave Neighborhoods in the Old South* (Chapel Hill: University of North Carolina Press, 2007); Thavolia Glymph, *Out of the House of Bondage: The Transformation of the Plantation Household* (Cambridge: Cambridge University Press, 2008); Marisa Fuentes, *Dispossessed Lives: Enslaved Women, Violence, and the Archive* (Philadelphia: University of Pennsylvania Press, 2018); and *Slavery in the City: Architecture and Landscapes of Urban Slavery in North America* (Charlottesville: University of Virginia Press, 2017).

106. For example, Katherine McKittrick discusses the Underground Railroad and making these invisible maps visible in chapter 1, *Demonic Grounds*.

JESSICA LARSON

The Black Built Environment of Benevolence in New York's Tenderloin District

Comparative Architectural Approaches to Race, Reform, and Discipline, 1865–1910

ABSTRACT

In 1901, a police precinct in Manhattan's Tenderloin District leveraged the eviction of their neighbor, the New York Colored Mission, and had the institution's building seized via eminent domain. The Colored Mission, founded by White Quakers in 1871, was purpose-built to serve the city's growing Black population at a moment when nearly every charitable institution in Manhattan excluded the non-White from aid. This eviction was part of a long and increasingly aggressive pattern of intimidation directed by the police toward the neighborhood's Black residents. However, the Colored Mission was not the only institution of its kind in the neighborhood. Just several lots to its east was the St. Philip's Parish House, a mission founded and built in 1895 by one of the most prominent Black congregations in the city. St. Philip's Parish House was roughly triple the size of the Colored Mission and signified the development of a coordinated Black-led effort to direct charity's response to Black poverty. This article examines and compares the architectural strategies employed by each mission and considers how the social services included in the institutions' differing designs facilitated differing approaches to racial progress. Further, this article positions and contextualizes the institutions within a complex landscape of segregation, racial violence, and urban development.

In 1907, the New York police department opened the newest node in their efforts to physically demarcate their expanding control over Manhattan: the Twenty-Third Police Precinct station house on West Thirtieth Street (Figure 1). Located in the heart of Manhattan's Tenderloin District, this new station house was hailed by the police commissioner as "the most important precinct in New York, if not the United States, or probably in the world."[1] Since the 1880s, the Tenderloin had been considered the most notorious concentration of vice in the city; it was also the most predominant Black neighborhood in Manhattan. Variously referred to as the Colored District, African Broadway, and Negro Bohemia, among other more inflammatory terms, much of the

Black cultural life that would later proliferate in Harlem found its roots in the Tenderloin.[2] As such, the police presence in the neighborhood was entwined with the development of racialized policing in late nineteenth- and early twentieth-century New York. To be sure, the new station house's architecture conveyed the perceived severity of the police's mission within the neighborhood. Designed by architect R. Thomas Short following years of heated input from precinct officials, the station house was constructed to mirror the architecture of a "warlike armory," one that could visually convey the precinct's intent to bring the Tenderloin's residents under the heel of the police department.[3] Some commentators questioned, or even mocked, this grandiosity. A

Figure 1. The Twenty-Third Police Precinct (Tenderloin) station house at 134–138 West Thirtieth Street, designed by architect R. Thomas Short, 1906–7. Photograph reproduced in *Architectural Record* vol. 30, no. 2 (July–December 1911): 183.

critic from the *Architectural Record* wrote with exasperation, "Why all this pother of warlike parade about the exterior of a station? [. . .] Why fortification? Why military architecture?," noting that the precinct's previous building, sited directly across the street from the new station house, had never experienced any attacks that might warrant such an extreme architectural response.[4]

To the Twenty-Third Police Precinct, however, the reason was clear: the new station house was the culmination of a building campaign that sought to transform the built environment of the Tenderloin—roughly bounded by West Twenty-Third Street to West Forty-Second Street between Sixth and Eighth Avenues—to reflect and defend claims to urban space by White city dwellers and business interests. This conflict transpired through clashes between the police and Black residents of the neighborhood, but its most physical expression was the result of the relationships between the police and Black reform institutions on West Thirtieth Street. This article examines the charitable and architectural programs of two institutions founded to serve Black relief seekers—the White-run New York Colored Mission and the Black-run St. Philip's Parish House—and considers how their divergent approaches to Black poverty materialized in their architectural designs. Building on arguments advanced by reform historian Linda Gordon, architectural historian Marta Gutman, and other scholars, this analysis contends that while White and Black reform movements shared similar motivations and programming, they differed in their strategies and successes; these distinctions can be read into the architectural choices of the Colored Mission and St. Philip's Parish House.[5]

Ultimately, St. Philip's relocated to Harlem, where the church expanded upon the spatial and reform practices it developed in the Tenderloin, while the Colored Mission was forced to relocate one block east following the police's seizure and destruction of their building. In studying these two institutions alongside the broader racial context of the Tenderloin, this article seeks to understand how reformers' differing ideologies of racial uplift were made spatial, as well as to interpret how larger hegemonic forces obstructed efforts to establish Black centers of benevolence and self-support. Further, this research expresses the ways in which, through the construction of Pennsylvania Station, the early twentieth-century modernization of Manhattan helped give birth to policies that entwined business and police interests to remap the Black landscape in favor of expanded White commercial interests. These precedents challenge the notion that New York City's principles of urban renewal were an outgrowth of mid-twentieth-century responses to concentrated blight or novel race relations following the Great Migration.

The New York Colored Mission and the Crisis of Black Migration to the North

The New York Colored Mission was originally created by White Quakers in 1865 with the specific intent of addressing the needs of arriving southern migrants in the wake of slavery.[6] When the Colored Mission was founded in 1865, Manhattan's Black population was primarily concentrated in an area of Greenwich Village popularly—and perhaps mockingly—termed Little Africa. Though small, this enclave was concentrated just south of Washington Square; in this area, Black residents were within walking distance of their places of employment, which were generally in domestic service or manual labor.[7] Following the Civil War, formerly enslaved Black southerners began to migrate to the North, with New York City's Black population doubling within a thirty-year span.[8] Compared to the simultaneous flood of White European immigrants, this growth in the Black population was still small, hovering at about 2 percent of the city's total population until the Great Migration. However, this influx meant that segregated Black neighborhoods were able to develop more fully.[9] While many Black migrants began to settle in the Tenderloin beginning in roughly 1880, in 1865 the area was not yet proximal to the majority of the Black population. Though it was developed, largely with buildings associated with manufacturing, it was not yet as dense as the more populated downtown.

In 1866, after having temporarily occupied five different locations, including a repurposed saloon and a room above a blacksmith's shop, the Colored Mission began to make plans for a building fund. Through women-led fundraising efforts, the bulk of the necessary money was secured, which was supplemented by donations and subscriptions. Though the organization originally intended to rent an existing property, no landlord could be found that was willing to allow their building to be used in service of the Black poor; the institution had garnered the name "Nigger School" by neighborhood residents who did not want it in their vicinity.[10] By 1868 the organization was able to purchase the lot at 135 West Thirtieth Street and plans were drafted for the creation of a purpose-built mission (Figure 2).[11] To fund the charitable work of the mission, the upper two stories of the five-story building were rented out to a Masonic lodge and the first story and basement were reserved for use as commercial spaces. This left only the second and third floors to be used by the institution. Originally, the second story was occupied by the Sabbath School and was used for religious meetings; an infant class was located on the same floor, with movable dividers separating it from the religious area. The third story was divided so that one room could be variously used as a Free Reading Room, a Free Intelligence Office (i.e., an employment bureau), and an office for the missionaries. Finally, living quarters were included for the mission's janitor and his family.[12]

Though very few institutions existed in New York City to assist Blacks, and nearly all White charities refused to open their doors to them, the Colored Mission had two sister institutions: the Colored Home for the Aged and Indigent, founded in 1839, and the Colored Orphan Asylum, founded in 1836. Both had comparatively large institutional buildings and, like the Colored Mission, were located a distance from antebellum centers of Black life. The construction of these two institutions had been facilitated by support from the city through the granting of municipal land, an offer not extended to the Colored Mission. In moves that were vocally disparaged by a number of White benevolent associations, which questioned why poor Blacks were prioritized over needy Whites, the city granted sections of Manhattan's Common Lands for the creation of the two institutions, with the justification that such endeavors would lessen Black dependence upon public institutions such as the almshouse.[13] While the Colored Home and Colored Orphan Asylum were founded prior to national Emancipation, the Colored Mission's purpose was entangled in postbellum questions of continued Black dependence upon White support. In the instances of the Colored Home and Colored Orphan Asylum, the case for the inmates constituting the "worthy poor" was an easier one to make. The Colored Home was founded to primarily serve elderly former slaves and sailors—sympathetic figures who had lived lives of service. Similarly, the children of the Colored Orphan Asylum were not yet capable of self-support.[14] These conditions were not a given for those seeking help from the Colored Mission.

To be sure, the memory of the 1863 draft riots was on the minds of the Colored Mission's Quaker founders. During the events, Blacks were scapegoated throughout Manhattan as anger among the White working class grew in response to the requirement for men to join the Union Army in the ongoing Civil War. Black homes, businesses, and churches were razed, as well as, most famously, the Colored Orphan Asylum's building on Fifth Avenue. With many Whites having been so vehemently against city funds supporting the land allotments given to the Asylum, the orphanage's grand, classical style building was considered disproportionally nice for its purposes of serving poor Black children (Figure 3). The orphanage was burned to the ground, its

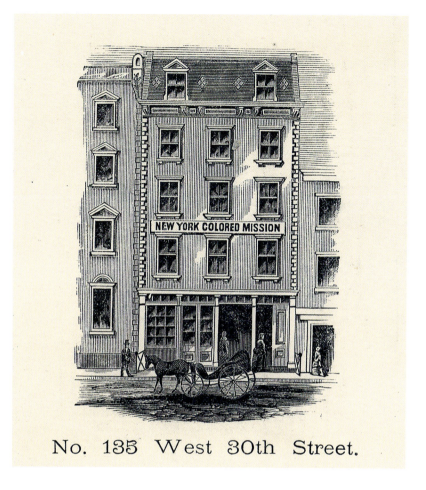

Figure 2. The New York Colored Mission's building at 135 West Thirtieth Street, printed on the frontispiece of the mission's annual report for 1876. Courtesy of the Schomburg Center for Research in Black Culture; Manuscripts, Archives and Rare Books Division, New York Public Library.

Figure 3. The Colored Orphan Asylum's building on Fifth Avenue, destroyed during the 1863 draft riots. From *Booth's History of New York*, vol. 7 (New York: W.R.C. Clark, 1867). Courtesy of the New York Public Library Digital Collections.

furniture smashed, and all surrounding trees, landscaping, and fences uprooted and destroyed. As such, its destruction was both a very real, physical attack against charity for Blacks and a violently symbolic gesture.[15] This reaction against the Asylum's building must have informed the Colored Mission's choice to fund a more modest structure.

The spatial organization of the mission's building articulated the early priorities of the institution: religious learning, which would have entailed literacy training, the proper rearing of children, and, most crucially, employment (Figures 4 and 5). As with many naïve White northerners, the founders of the mission had mistakenly believed that Emancipation would lead to Black northerners moving South. With the steady increase in the city's Black population, the Colored Mission's reformers sought to both exploit what they viewed as their clients' natural predisposition to service and fill occupations that were desperately needed in New York City. The mission's employment bureau, then, primarily served to find domestic work for Black relief seekers, particularly women. The mission asserted that Black women were seeking employment in "saloons and houses of ill fame" instead of in plentiful domestic labor jobs. That such work paid considerably more than domestic work was, seemingly, not an important detail to the organization's reformers. This ignorance aligns with arguments made by historian Alice Kessler-Harris regarding middle-class reformers' motives for training wage-earning women in trades like domestic service or sewing, which were considered skills that would then support women's familial duties.[16] The Colored Mission's hope was that the services offered would do the work of acculturating Black women into expectations of propriety, reifying structures of race and class while pushing the poor off of charitable support, and, ultimately, shuttering the doors of the neighborhood's institutions of vice. These expectations were informed by the mission's Quaker beliefs, which charged that adherence to Christian principles and the elimination of sinful temptations were necessary to escape poverty.[17]

The mission's work became more complex as the institution garnered expanded resources. It added a small lodging room for women in 1874 to provide Black women and girls—those newly arrived from the South and with no kin in the

Figure 4. Prayer meeting in the New York Colored Mission's West Thirtieth Street building, printed in the mission's annual report for 1901. Courtesy of the Schomburg Center for Research in Black Culture; Manuscripts, Archives and Rare Books Division, New York Public Library.

Figure 5. The New York Colored Mission's employment bureau in their West Thirtieth Street building, printed in the mission's annual report for 1901. A White woman reformer for the institution sits behind a desk to assist Black clients seeking job placements. Courtesy of the Schomburg Center for Research in Black Culture; Manuscripts, Archives and Rare Books Division, New York Public Library.

city—with temporary housing; ideally, at the same time, the mission's employment bureau would help these women find steady work.[18] Initially, only twelve beds were provided, likely dormitory style; by 1891 this number grew to forty-five beds. A new bathroom supplied by hot and cold water was added for the women, as well as a space for laundry with stationary washtubs; lodgers were charged fifteen cents a night.[19] In perspective, Black women working in occupations such as domestic service in 1880s New York could expect to make at most four dollars a week. Though still a significant portion of a woman's weekly wages, this price was consistent with those demanded by comparable lodging houses in the area for White boarders.[20] As was the standard nature of lodging houses, the mission's lodgers would have been responsible for their own meals and expected (or possibly required) to vacate the space during the day in an effort to encourage employment. In the evenings, Bible verse readings were encouraged in the lodging room. As expressed by the mission's reformers, a careful balance needed to be struck between the evocation of a homelike, enriching environment and a place that did not invite idle lingering.[21]

No similar accommodations were extended to Black men at the Colored Mission. Though the institution hoped to raise the funds to construct a separate building to serve as a men's lodging house, the plans never materialized and the project was seemingly abandoned early in the mission's history. The focus on women came from several related factors. As sociologist Theda Skocpol has demonstrated, late nineteenth-century reform contended that women were inherently weaker and less self-sufficient than men and thus more in need of support.[22] However, the Colored Mission's focus on women was also largely due to worries over the predominance of sex or saloon work in the Tenderloin. As phrased by historian Timothy J. Gilfoyle, "Sex in the Tenderloin was also a racial affair."[23] By the 1880s, the neighborhood was associated with Black prostitution, with reformers and other White New Yorkers particularly incensed by continuous accounts of mixed-race prostitution published nearly daily in newspapers.[24] Although the reality was far less sensational, such coverage belied the networks of support for the Black poor in the neighborhood and bolstered White interests in removing undesirable residents in favor of expanded commercial interests. These accounts rarely noted the number of vocal Black reformers or aid seekers invested in addressing the structural causes of sex work.

St. Philip's Parish House and Real Estate as Reform

By the 1890s, the Tenderloin was indisputably regarded as the center of Manhattan's Black cultural life, though both White and Black city dwellers worried over the neighborhood's seemingly unwieldy growth. Though the majority of the city's most prominent Black churches had migrated from Greenwich Village to the Tenderloin, little could be done to change the perception of the neighborhood as a concentration of immorality.[25] One White commentator wrote, "That the Tenderloin is infested with depraved and vicious Negroes is obvious to pedestrians who by day note the groups of flashily dressed colored men who swagger idly about the street corners, or who by night are accosted or even held up by the female associates of these loathsome wretches."[26] A number of prominent Black figures shared this disdain for the neighborhood and viewed Black Tenderloiners as a hindrance to racial progress. Black writer Paul Laurence Dunbar excoriated the Tenderloin's residents in an 1897 article published in *The Sun,* writing:

> One looks at the crowds of idle, shiftless negroes that throng [the Tenderloin] and the question must arise, What is to be done with them, what is to be done for them, if they are to be prevented from inoculating our civilization with the poison of their lives? [. . .] Here and there sits a weak, ineffectual little mission, doing its little best for the people around it, but altogether as inadequate as a gauze fan in the furnace heats of hell.[27]

Black reformers evinced prejudices similar to their White counterparts, but with different motivations and different architectural solutions. One such figure central to Black reform efforts in the Tenderloin, and later Harlem, was Reverend Hutchens C. Bishop, who became rector of St. Philip's Protestant Episcopal Church in 1886. Like many other middle-class and elite Black reformers, Bishop's desire for class identification sometimes took precedence over racial solidarity. The reform work undertaken by St. Philip's in the Tenderloin reflected these concerns and, like the Colored Mission, sought to manage the living conditions of newly arrived Black migrants.

St. Philip's began as a part of Lower Manhattan's historic Trinity Church. In 1810, the number of Black attendees at Trinity, who were required to hold separate services, had become so numerous that the church's building was no longer sufficient and additional rooms were rented in nearby buildings.[28] With mounting tensions between the splinter congregation and the all-White Trinity, the Black congregants officially organized as St. Philip's Protestant Episcopal Church in 1818 and for decades rented several different locations before finally purchasing an existing Presbyterian church in the Tenderloin on West Twenty-Fifth Street in 1886.[29] Prior to this, in 1872, while still sited downtown, St. Philip's had established a parish house at 127 West Thirtieth Street, just four lots to the east of the Colored Mission, and one year after the mission's construction. The land at 115–131 West Thirtieth Street had been gifted to St. Philip's by Trinity Church, which purchased the land sometime in the early nineteenth century, likely to be used as a burial ground.[30] A three-story frame home with a two-story lean-to was erected at 127 West Thirtieth Street, which was rented out to White families until 1872. By 1890, an additional one-story lean-to was added (Figure 6).[31]

In 1872, a group of some of the most prominent women congregants of St. Philip's petitioned to convert the frame house and use it as a care residence for the church's elderly women. Called St. Philip's Parish Home, the church's women reformers managed the institution's programming, including its fundraising and social events.[32] Though women were not the primary figureheads of the organization, as was also customary in the Colored Mission's hierarchy, contemporary commentary makes it clear that this was a women-led venture; one publication stated that the institution "while not originated alone by women, [was] founded mainly by them, and [has] always been indebted for their maintenance largely to the acts of self-sacrifice, the liberality of females."[33]

In line with the architectural progression of other Black-run institutions, what began as an instance of adaptive reuse evolved into a purpose-built structure.[34] By the early 1890s, St. Philip's had grown significantly in terms of both number of congregants and accrued wealth. To keep pace with the city's expanding White benevolent empire, and to assist the Tenderloin's growing Black population, the church recognized the need to provide a more encompassing array of social welfare services. Under the direction of the ambitious Hutchens C. Bishop, the old age home was relocated to a former schoolhouse in the Bronx in 1896.[35] Coinciding with these developments, the church began preparations for what was to replace the former site on West Thirtieth Street. St. Philip's hired the architectural firm Fowler & Hough to design the new Parish House building.[36] The original renderings for the building show an ambitiously ornamented structure, complete with three stories, a raised basement that appears to have been designed for commercial purposes, and a tall central spire surmounting a square tower (Figure 7). This design was likely deemed impractical on several fronts: while the enlarged spire signaled the religious affiliation of the institution, it left little room for social work,

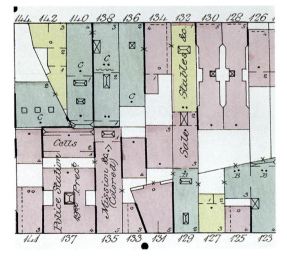

Figure 6. Section of an 1890 Sanborn map showing the institutions on West Thirtieth Street. St. Philip's original Parish Home, which served elderly Black women from the congregation, is shown at 127; the yellow coloring indicates that it was frame construction. From "Manhattan," vol. 5 (1890), double page plate no. 88. Courtesy of the New York Public Library Digital Collections.

and the original entryway also occupied valuable commercial space on the ground floor. The design of the Parish House that was ultimately built did away with the spire and opted instead for an additional story, as well as a far less sweeping entrance to make way for commercial units (Figure 8).

Though photographs of the Parish House's exterior present the building, which covered three lots, as a unified structure, fire insurance maps show that on each of the three lots was a separate structure, with party walls between each building (Figure 9). As few extant sources provide any detailed information regarding the uses of the Parish House, architectural analysis offers insight. The center structure at 127 West Thirtieth Street filled its entire lot, with no room left to accommodate air shafts. The two buildings flanking this, at 125 and 129 West Thirtieth Street, however, included air shafts on both sides of the structures, as well as rear lots. This indicates that these two structures were used as housing, while the central portion was reserved for reform work. The plans for 125 and 129 West Thirtieth Street would have been governed by the Tenement House Act of 1879 (aka the Old Law), which required new residential buildings to limit lot coverage to 65 percent. The law also required that any room used for sleeping in either a tenement or lodging house include a window. And, as required by the first tenement house law, enacted in 1867, a second means of egress was requisite for each unit, which usually took the form of a fire escape.[37]

Based on these housing code regulations, the buildings at 125 and 129 West Thirtieth Street were used as apartments. As seen in photographs, the way the fire escapes in these two structures were positioned indicates that each had two street-facing units; presumably, two units were also positioned at the rear and had fire escape exits to the back lot. No fire escapes are shown on the exterior of the building at 127 West Thirtieth Street. The 1900 federal census recorded that seven families lived at 125 West Thirtieth Street while nine families lived at 129 West Thirtieth Street. Curiously, while the majority of these families were Black and from the South, two White families resided there.[38] Tenants' occupations were categorized as either labor, service, or domestic work. Men held jobs such as waiters or bellhops, while women were laundresses or domestic servants. Based on mentions in the Black press of social events hosted by residents, tenants were often members of St. Philip's Church and not of, as Bishop would say, "a class of people that [he did] not care to be particularly identified with."[39]

St. Philip's development of housing for Black tenants was not a purely charitable endeavor. As with the church's later and greatly expanded real estate dealings in Harlem, this was both a shrewd business move and an effort to define a Black middle class through establishing a foothold in the city's real estate. St. Philip's had long been considered the most elite Black church in New York City and one that prided itself on primarily serving "blueblood" congregants—descendants of free Blacks from before slavery ended in New York in 1827.[40] Thus, the church leadership's emphasis on apartment rentals over short-term lodging, as the Colored Mission had chosen, spoke to the congregation's larger interest in assisting those who were already upwardly mobile.

Figure 7. Original renderings for the St. Philip's Parish House, designed by architects Fowler & Hough, 1896. From *Building: An Architectural Monthly* 25, no. 11 (September 12, 1896).

This practice followed the precedents established by St. Philip's parent church, Trinity. Beginning in the early eighteenth century, Trinity began acquiring and developing massive land holdings in Lower Manhattan; by the late nineteenth century, Trinity was the largest landlord in the city and a notorious slumlord.[41] Outcries against the conditions of Trinity-owned tenements were particularly heated in the 1890s, when Trinity very publicly fought against legal mandates to include water access in their buildings, arguing that such provisions did not constitute a public good.[42]

The original parcel of land given to St. Philip's by Trinity stretched from 115 to 131 West Thirtieth Street, with only lots 125 to 129 used for the Parish House; the remaining six lots were rented for both residential and commercial use, mostly by Whites. Like Trinity, St. Philip's approached their real estate holdings as a business venture separate from their religious mission. In the 1900 federal census, nearly all tenants occupying St. Philip's residential properties were White.[43] As St. Philip's Tenderloin records are sparse it is difficult to claim conclusively that their rental properties provided the revenue for the construction of the 1896 Parish House, though such a move aligns with the church's later financial choices in Harlem.[44]

While the wings of the Parish House at 125 and 129 West Thirtieth Street were used as apartments, the central structure at 127 West Thirtieth Street was used for reform work. No records clearly define the institution's programing, but evidence indicates that the Parish House focused on work with children, particularly young boys. Programs for adolescent boys included a glee club, acting classes, and industrial training. Perhaps most notably, athletics such as boxing and track, as well as a championship basketball team called the St. Christopher Club, were the institution's most celebrated activities, and the Parish House included a gymnasium for them.[45]

This program differed significantly from the Colored Mission's women-centered approach, which underscored the familial, social, and employment duties of Black women over expectations for men. Certainly, women were still central to the decisions of the Parish House; a photograph of the interior office spaces shows two women working at a desk, one typing while the other writes by hand (Figure 10). The room, which features movable partition doors to enhance or close off space, is shown carefully decorated with a chinoiserie vase on the fireplace

Figure 8. The completed version of St. Philip's Parish House, 125–129 West Thirtieth Street. Photograph taken by the Byron Company, ca. 1897. Courtesy of the Museum of the City of New York.

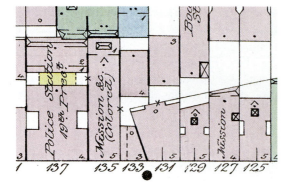

Figure 9. Section of an 1898 Sanborn Fire Insurance Map showing the Twenty-Third Police Precinct (137), the New York Colored Mission (135), and the St. Philip's Parish House (125–129). At 127, marked "Mission," the structure takes up its entire lot space, while those at 127 and 129 include airshafts and the requisite undeveloped space in the rear lot. From "Manhattan," vol. 5 (1898), double page plate no. 88. Courtesy of the New York Public Library Digital Collections.

Figure 10. Women shown performing administrative work in the St. Philip's Parish House. Photograph taken by the Byron Company, ca. 1897. Courtesy of the Museum of the City of New York.

mantel and framed prints adorning the walls and bookshelves. The women, equally well composed, wear modest dresses that convey the importance of reform to the early professionalization of women in bureaucratic work.

Perhaps in part because of the focus on young boys rather than women, the Parish House garnered a reputation for permissiveness regarding activities generally abhorred by reformers. At a conference at the Hampton Institute (later Hampton University) in Virginia, Bishop stated that the Parish House allowed young boys to play cards and billiards, as well as smoke cigarettes, in an effort to attract otherwise wayward youth. This admission was met with anger from other attendees, with one woman declaring, "It's a good thing he's a'Pisc'palian. Ef he was a real preacher, a Baptis' I mean, he'd be carried out yonder in Hampton Roads. Yo' hear me."[46] Though the Parish House's approach was evidently not well received by some critics, this was clearly not a viewpoint held by all Black reformers. In a letter to the editor of *The Sun*, one of the city's leading Black reformers, Victoria Earle Matthews, admonished the newspaper for its continually scandalous coverage of the Tenderloin, reporting that implied that the criminality of the neighborhood was indicative of the entire race. Matthews singled out St. Philip's Parish House as an example of how Black-run institutions were better equipped to meet their community's needs than comparable White institutions, largely because the Parish House focused less on discipline and more on the cultivation of social bonds.[47]

In sum, the Tenderloin's two most prominent charitable institutions—both built to serve the city's growing Black population—prioritized different components of reform and their buildings' designs expressed these differences. In respect to housing, the efforts undertaken by the Colored Mission and St. Philip's likely catered to very different demographics. The Colored Mission's lodging house primarily served working-poor women, new to the city and in need of work and temporary shelter, while St. Philip's cultivated their experience and background in property management to build apartments for poor or lower-middle-class tenants. In the 1900 federal census, residents of the Parish House are listed as being employed in positions ranging from low-wage occupations such as laundresses to better paying jobs such as hairdressers.[48] At a moment when White landlords were notoriously exploitative of Black tenants, the prospect of Black-controlled housing was very appealing to Black Tenderloiners. Further, as historian Kevin McGruder has argued in regard to St. Philip's strategies in Harlem, the development of Black church property in Black neighborhoods was entwined with efforts to prevent harassment and displacement by White residents.[49] While St. Philip's reform choices reflected their larger mission to foreground aspirations toward middle-class stability and, like the Colored Mission, reward those who abided by the traditional family structure, the church's strategy offered the hope of class advancement that was not constrained by the demands of White reform.

Penn Station and Police Incursions in the Landscape of Black Reform

St. Philip's was right to consider the ways in which property ownership and development might offer a defense against displacement. Following years of escalating tensions between the Tenderloin's Black and White residents, heightened by the actions of the district's police, the New York Colored Mission was evicted from their building in 1901 and forced to relocate and rebuild one block west. While St. Philip's was likely not threatened with the seizure of their building by the city as the Colored Mission was, St. Philip's investment in real estate and experiments in housing facilitated the congregation's ability to accumulate enough wealth to purchase land and buildings and relocate to Harlem. The church was still, in a sense, a victim of the neighborhood's changing conditions. The Parish House's land, alongside the church's other West Thirtieth Street properties, was sold to developers in 1911 to construct office space for the newly opened Pennsylvania Station (Penn Station). As many of their congregants' homes were leveled to make way for the

railway, the church had few options other than to follow their flock northward. The construction of the train station, alongside fallout from the Tenderloin riots of 1900, wherein Black residents and their property were attacked following the murder of a White police officer, were the most crucial factors in the migration of Black Tenderloin residents to San Juan Hill and Harlem. When considered together, the siting of Penn Station and police efforts to manage inhabitants of the Tenderloin sought to deliberately rid the area of Black residents and renew the neighborhood's reputation as a place for White commerce, leisure, and modern industry.

Though sites across Lower Manhattan were considered and prioritized in the planning of Penn Station, the choice of eight acres between Seventh and Eighth Avenues between Thirty-First and Thirty-Third Streets was surprising. With many factors to consider, no logistically ideal areas would escape wholesale clearance. Thankfully for the station's planners and city officials, there already existed a neighborhood widely considered a blight on the city's progress. As articulated by a local realtor to Samuel Rea, the president of the Pennsylvania Railroad Company, "Seventh Avenue has been for many years considered to be like a Chinese wall on the west side of the city south of 42nd St. [. . .] on and beyond which no respectable man or woman could safely go. It is known as filled with thugs, bums, and wicked negroes."[50] As argued by architectural and urban historian Hilary Ballon, this destruction of huge swaths of the Tenderloin and removal of undesirable groups in favor of Penn Station constituted the first urban renewal project of twentieth-century Manhattan, a contention bolstered by the railroad's choice to bar the processing of new immigrants at the station. While the area designated for demolition was not targeted exclusively because of its high volume of Black residents, their presence in the Tenderloin contributed to the notion that the area was expendable or, better yet, should be eradicated. Douglas Robinson, president of the real estate company contracted by the railroad company, justified the choice, stating, "The buildings in the Terminal zone were occupied by many negroes, saloons, dance halls, gambling joints, and for many other purposes which made the work of those who did the buying not only difficult, but also often dangerous."[51]

The financial and municipal interests that governed the selection of the Tenderloin for Penn Station reinforced police efforts to push out Black residents. The original Twenty-Third Police Precinct station house was designed by the official architect to the police department, Nathaniel D. Bush, and was constructed one lot to the west of the Colored Mission at 137 West Thirtieth Street in 1869, one year following the mission's purchase of their lot (Figure 11).[52] After years of escalating tensions, violent conflicts between White and Black Tenderloiners and the police came to a head in August 1900 when a Black man, Arthur Harris, killed a White police officer, Robert Thorpe, in self-defense after Thorpe attempted to wrongfully arrest Harris's common-law wife, May Enoch, for prostitution. As news of Thorpe's death spread, Whites, reportedly with assistance from the police, initiated violent attacks on Blacks throughout the Tenderloin and destroyed Black-owned property.[53]

Following the 1900 Tenderloin riots, efforts increased to conform the geography of the Tenderloin to the expectations of the city's White political and economic leaders. These actions were led by William McAdoo, New York City's police commissioner from 1904 to 1906. McAdoo, a former congressman from New Jersey, made no secret about his desires or plans to tighten the police's grip on the city's most criminal neighborhoods, with the Tenderloin being a specific concern. Plans to replace the West Thirtieth Street station house had been underway since 1898, prior to McAdoo's tenure. Called the "Most Important Police Precinct in America" by the *New York Times,* the Health Board had long condemned the building for its conditions and plans had steadily been underway since the late 1890s to either renovate or replace the station house. That the New York Colored Mission occupied the lot directly beside the station house offered a solution to the police's architectural problems, as well as an opportunity to disrupt a site of poor Black congregation and upward mobility. No evi-

Figure 11. The Twenty-Third Police Precinct's first station house at 137 West Thirtieth Street, built in 1869 and designed by architect Nathaniel D. Bush. To the right, a small portion of the New York Colored Mission can be seen. Reproduced in Augustine E. Costello, *Our Police Protectors: History of the New York Police from the Earliest Period to the Present Time* (New York: Cadmus Press, 1884).

dence can confirm the motivations of the police, but contextual information indicates that their seizure of the Colored Mission's building was not born out of a purely practical solution to their need for new facilities. That the Tenderloin Police Precinct was notoriously racist and hostile toward the neighborhood's Black residents was well documented, as was the growth of their aggression toward Black New Yorkers following 1900.[54]

In 1898, the city issued an order of seizure of the Colored Mission's lots via eminent domain, nominally for the purpose of enlarging the existing stationhouse.[55] The building, referred to as the "nigger mission" by the West Thirtieth Street police, was not officially turned over to the precinct until 1902; seemingly, the police did not begin to forcibly push for the consolidation until after the 1900 Tenderloin riots. Mentions of the police's takeover of the building do not appear in the mission's annual reports until 1900, at which point the institution began to officially search for a new site.[56] The city compensated the mission for the purchase of two new lots one block west at 225–227 West Thirtieth Street, though they did not cover the costs of new building construction (Figure 12).[57] The mission's move required both the adaptation of existing spaces and the construction of a new, purpose-built structure. At 227 West Thirtieth Street was a three-story

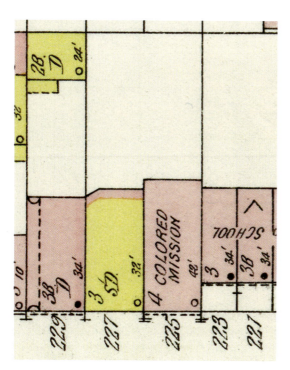

Figure 12. The new location of the New York Colored Mission at 225–227 West Thirtieth Street. The yellow frame structure at 227 was an existing house converted to a lodging house by the mission. The building at 225 marked "Colored Mission" was purpose-built by architect John Russell Pope, 1902. These new lots provided ample yard space for children's activities. From "Manhattan," vol. 5 (1911), plate no. 21. Courtesy of the New York Public Library Digital Collections.

frame home, built in 1856, with added masonry extensions.[58] Once owned by the Colored Mission, this home was converted to the mission's lodging house, which was presumably expanded given the much greater space afforded by the house than in the institution's previous building.

The neighboring lot purchased by the Colored Mission at 225 West Thirtieth Street was occupied by a row house, which was torn down and replaced by the institution's new building, a five-story structure that mirrored the general spatial arrangement of the previous location but deviated in certain respects (Figure 13). This new building was designed by architect John Russell Pope, more famous for buildings such as the National Gallery of Art (1937–41) and the Jefferson Memorial in Washington, D.C. (1939–43).[59] Notable differences from the original building were the inclusion of a gymnasium in the basement and significantly more yard space, which was filled with playground equipment (Figure 14).

Though the Twenty-Third Precinct had stated their intention to use the Colored Mission's original building as an annex for either storage or sleeping quarters for officers, it was never used as such. The building fell into disrepair and became effectively unusable by 1904, when new plans were devised to construct a wholly new station house. In 1903, architect R. Thomas Short drafted plans for a new precinct house to replace the former one, which would extend into the former lots of the Colored Mission. McAdoo made no secret of his disdain for Short's proposal; in his memoirs, McAdoo wrote, "Outwardly it looked like a second-class apartment-house. It gave no suggestion of its official character, and the internal arrangements were more fanciful than practical. The architect had followed the usual lines with regard to these structures."[60] Under McAdoo's guidance, the plans were radically redrafted by Short to convey his understanding of what sort of architectural and ideological presence the police force should have in the Tenderloin. Plans to build over the existing lots were scrapped altogether, and the city provided the precinct with $170,000 to purchase the two lots directly across the street at 134–138 West Thirtieth Street, demolish the existing buildings on the site, and construct a new, grander station house.[61] Again, this plan required the seizure by eminent domain of a Black charitable institution, the St. Timothy's Baptist Church Mission at 136 West Thirtieth Street. This small mission had rented the second story of a former farmhouse, previously used as a saloon, since 1893. Little information exists to indicate what specific work the mission did, though it seems to have been mostly focused on children. Exasperated, the mission's figurehead, Reverend Richard R. Wilson, was quoted in *The Sun*:

> I don't know which way to turn . . . you see, we get our place of worship very cheap; only $27 a month. I've been looking around for another place, but they all cost so much money. We never could pay the rents asked. It takes the heart right out of me when I think of having to carry out those pews and song books and the organ. Where we will put them I am at a loss to say.[62]

As tenants and not owners, St. Timothy's was not extended the same sort of financial compensation by the city that the Colored Mission was offered.

McAdoo's directives for the layout of the new station house, for the most part, amounted to choices that restricted the transparency of police actions: the front entrance obscured the process of bringing arrestees from patrol wagons into the station house so that the "perp walk" was no longer visible to onlookers. This event had previously and notoriously been used as an opportunity for officers to "even the score" by dragging prisoners over the stationhouse's stone steps, a spectacle McAdoo hoped to avoid. Additionally, the new stationhouse's reception room did not accommodate the previously large numbers of reporters who gathered to report on arrests, and more cells were included.[63] As noted by the *Architectural Record*, it was the façade that drew the most public attention, however. The publication's critic puzzled over the choice to shoddily replicate a "Military Gothic" defensive structure simply to "throw a scare" into generally petty criminals, with no real features that would be useful in the unlikely event of an assault (see Figure 1). To many onlookers, the design conveyed an unnecessary gesture of intimidation, disproportionate to the purpose of the precinct.[64]

Why McAdoo and the Twenty-Third Precinct focused on disciplining public space in the Tenderloin cannot be entirely attributed to efforts to curtail Black networks of support or social advancement, but that the police associated the criminality of the Tenderloin with Blackness is reflected in writings by McAdoo. In a lengthy screed against Black Tenderloiners published in *Harper's Weekly*, McAdoo wrote:

> One of the most troublesome and dangerous characters with which the police have to deal is the Tenderloin type of negro. In the male species this is the overdressed, flashy, bejeweled loafer, gambler, and, in many instances, general criminal. [...] The negro loafer is a more dangerous character than the white cadet, as he is subject to violent fits of jealously, and when filled with the raw alcohol which is dispensed in the neighborhood, murder comes natural and easy to him.[65]

Regarding Black women, McAdoo contended that "the vicious and drunken colored woman differs somewhat from her White sister in that she, too, in a paroxysm of passion, and under the influence of liquor, is likely to use a weapon very freely, and not a few of them carry revolvers and razors."

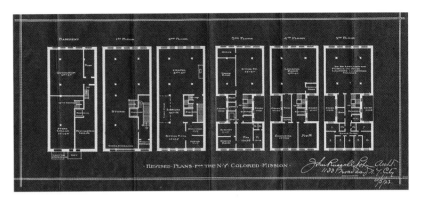

Figure 13. John Russell Pope's plans for the new New York Colored Mission building at 225 West Thirtieth Street, 1902. While similar to the spatial arrangement of the original building, this one featured a gymnasium in the basement and more individual rooms for classes. Courtesy of the Haverford College Quaker & Special Collections Library.

Figure 14. Photograph of children in the New York Colored Mission's new yard space, printed in the mission's 1901 annual report. Courtesy of the Schomburg Center for Research in Black Culture; Manuscripts, Archives and Rare Books Division, New York Public Library.

This statement echoed those made by journalists and other city officials, who claimed that the Tenderloin was plagued by roving groups of Black women who regularly assaulted and robbed White men.[66]

As a solution to Black crime in the Tenderloin, McAdoo called for the police to centralize power around the Tenderloin Precinct to expand investigations into mixed-race businesses.[67] Certainly, McAdoo's prejudices and how they impacted his policies were well known in the Black community. In 1905, the Black publication the *New York Age* wrote, "The enthusiastic preference shown Afro-Americans by the police—as marks for their clubs and objects of arrests—is scandalous, but no longer strange; that is, since we learn that the rank and file of the force is but putting into practice the opinions which obtain [from McAdoo]."[68] McAdoo's approaches to policing the Tenderloin, and how they materialized in the built environment, would have been understood as entwined with White anxieties over the increasingly visible presence of Manhattan's Black population and impulses to restrict the proliferation of Black cultural, social, and economic advancements. These spatial choices aligned with the motives for the railroad's construction to the west of Seventh Avenue, which explicitly sought to push Black residents and institutions of vice either farther to the western edge of Manhattan or to the north, with the expectation that the growing shopping district surrounding Herald Square would expand into sections of the Tenderloin that were formerly in disrepair.[69]

Conclusion

The Twenty-Third Precinct's new station house opened in 1908, and the lots on which the original building and Colored Mission were located were soon cleared and lay vacant as the city debated their future. On her first day in office in 1913, the city's first female Commissioner of Corrections, Katharine Bement Davis, met with McAdoo to discuss the construction of a women's court and prison on the lots.[70] Though architects Griffin & Wynkoop were the designers of the proposed building, Davis made known her central involvement in the project, with *The Sun* reporting that she was "chiefly responsible for the interior arrangement" (Figure 15). Due primarily to financial and logistical issues, the structure was never built; if it had been, the fourteen-story structure would have reportedly been the tallest prison in the world. Davis, who had begun her career in the settlement house movement, viewed the women's prison project as an extension of Progressive reform efforts. In certain ways, the disciplinary approach to reform established by institutions like the Colored Mission directly led to such policies.[71]

In 1907, as the construction of the new Tenderloin station house was underway, St. Philip's began the process of relocating uptown, as other prominent Black churches had already done. In October of that year, the church's leadership authorized plans to organize the creation of a new reform institution on West 134th Street. Throughout 1908, Reverend Hutchens C. Bishop began to steadily purchase tenement buildings and row houses along West 133rd and 134th Streets, which had dropped in value as a result of overspeculation driven by the railway's expansion.[72] In 1909, the congregation sold off its West Thirtieth Street Parish House and other properties for $1,966 per frontage foot, as well as the West Twenty-Fifth Street church building. These sites were planned for office space for the newly opened Penn Station.[73] With the money raised through these property sales, St. Philip's purchased the two lots on West 133rd Street to construct their new parish house, and two lots on West 134th Street directly behind them for the church building. As a testament to the centrality of architecture to the church's mission of racial uplift, the firm of Tandy & Foster—two of the first Black architects in New York—were hired to design the church and parish house, for which Tandy earned the moniker "Harlem's architect" (Figure 16).[74]

Though St. Philip's had been buying up residential properties along West 133rd and 134th for several years in anticipation of the church's move, it was not until 1911 that the organization made its largest purchase. Facilitated by Black real estate brokers John E. Nail and Henry G. Parker and paid for with the funds secured through the sale of the Tenderloin properties, St. Philip's bought a row of ten modern apartment buildings, promptly evicted all White occupants, and rented out the units to Black tenants (Figure 17). This constituted the largest real estate deal involving Black property purchasers up until that time.[75] The acquisition of these residential properties, like the new parish house, extended the work that had originated on West Thirtieth Street and allowed for the church to fund a robust charity and reform program, as well as to provide quality housing to members of the congregation.

While St. Philip's and other Black institutions achieved lasting success in Harlem, many Black families, businesses, and charities never overcame the targeted destruction of the Tenderloin. The devastating consequences of increasing police encroachment into the lives and efforts

Figure 15. Rendering for the proposed Women's House of Detention by architects Griffin & Wynkoop, 1914. Purportedly, Katharine Bement Davis, the newly appointed and first female Commissioner of Corrections in New York City, had significant say over its design. If built, this would have replaced the former lots of the New York Colored Mission and original Twenty-Third Police Precinct station house, spanning 135–137 West Thirtieth Street. Courtesy of the Irma and Paul Milstein Division of United States History, Local History and Genealogy, New York Public Library.

Figure 16. Photograph of the new Harlem building for the St. Philip's Parish House, designed by architects Tandy & Foster, 1911. Printed in the Black-run *New York Age*, January 19, 1911, 8.

Figure 17. View of 107–145 West 135th Street, purchased by St. Philip's Episcopal Church in 1911 in partnership with Black realtors John E. Nail and Henry G. Parker. These were exclusively rented to Black tenants, continuing the practices that St. Philip's had developed in the Tenderloin. Courtesy of the Schomburg Center for Research in Black Culture, Photographs and Prints Division, New York Public Library.

of Black Tenderloiners, the expansion of infrastructure projects like Penn Station to meet the demands of a modernizing metropolis, and landlords' preference for renting to the mounting numbers of White immigrants in need of housing disrupted critical networks of Black support. The relocation of formerly Tenderloin-sited institutions uptown brought established forms of relief to new neighborhoods, yet the imbalance between organizations that would serve Black clients and those that were exclusive to the White poor persisted, even in Harlem.[76] In erasing an albeit flawed landscape of Black aspiration and benevolence, the city's hegemonic forces prioritized a vision of urban progress that expressed discipline and punishment spatially. Though a comparatively small episode in the larger history of both Black New York and Manhattan's development, these case studies demonstrate that the patterns of race-based displacement later adapted on a massive scale were in practice long before mid-century policies of urban renewal. Despite this unrelenting systemic erasure, Black reformers rebuilt and expanded their institutions in Harlem, drawing on lessons learned in the Tenderloin. These strategies translated into distinct architectural choices and fostered the charitable infrastructure necessary to support newcomers soon to arrive during the Great Migration.

AUTHOR BIOGRAPHY

Jessica Larson is a doctoral candidate in Art and Architectural History at the Graduate Center of the City University of New York. Her dissertation examines the architecture of Black charitable and reform institutions built in Manhattan between the Civil War and World War I.

ACKNOWLEDGMENTS

I would like to thank Marta Gutman, Robin Veder, Agnieszka Anna Ficek, and editors Michael J. Chiarappa and Margaret M. Grubiak for their thoughtful suggestions and comments. Thank you as well to staff at the Schomburg Center for Research in Black Culture and the Smithsonian American Art Museum for their research assistance. I presented a version of this paper at the 2022 Vernacular Architecture Forum Annual Conference in San Antonio, and I am grateful to those colleagues for their comments.

NOTES

1. William McAdoo, *Guarding a Great City* (New York: Harper & Bros., 1906), 93–95.

2. Robert M. Dowling, *Slumming in New York: From the Waterfront to Mythic Harlem* (Champaign: University of Illinois Press, 2007), 83; David Gilbert, *Products of Our Souls: Ragtime, Race, and the Birth of the Manhattan Musical Marketplace* (Chapel Hill: University of North Carolina Press, 2015), 23.

3. "Old 'Tenderloin' Station Awaiting Its Doom," *New York Times*, May 13, 1906, 4.

4. "Architectural Aberration—The Twenty-Third Precinct Police Station, New York," *Architectural Record* 30, no. 2 (July–December 1911), 181.

5. See Linda Gordon, "Black and White Visions of Welfare: Women's Welfare Activism, 1890–1945," *Journal of American History* 78, no. 2 (1991): 559–90; and Marta Gutman, *City for Children: Women, Architecture, and the Charitable Landscape of Oakland, 1830–1950* (Chicago: University of Chicago Press, 2014).

6. African Mission School Association, *A Mission School among the Colored People of New York* (New York, 1868), 3; "Conference of the Orthodox Friends," *New York Daily Herald*, June 2, 1872, 6.

7. Diana diZerega Wall, Nan A. Rothschild, and Cynthia Copeland, "Seneca Village and Little Africa: Two African American Communities in Antebellum New York City," *Historical Archaeology* 42, no. 1 (2008): 97–107.

8. Department of Commerce, Bureau of the Census, *Negro Population in the United States, 1790–1915* (Washington, D.C., 1968), 43–44.

9. Gilbert Osofsky, "Progressivism and the Negro: New York, 1900–1915," *American Quarterly* 16, no. 1 (Summer 1964): 153–54.

10. It should be noted that there was another school dedicated to Black children's education in the vicinity. This was the Colored School No. 4, located on West Seventeenth Street between Six and Seventh Avenues. The close proximity of these two institutions likely informed White residents' increasing animosity toward the Mission. Augustus Taber, "New York Colored Mission: The Beginning of Its Work," included in the *Annual Report of the New York Colored Mission* (New York, 1887).

11. African Mission School Association, *A Mission School for the Colored People of New York* (New York, 1868), 1.

12. *Annual Report of the New York Colored Mission* (New York, 1871), 5.

13. "Private Charities and Public Lands," *New Catholic World* 29 (New York, 1879): 132. The Colored Home, located on First Avenue between Sixty-Fourth and Sixty-Fifth Streets, was originally intended to house elderly Blacks but was later charged by the city to also shelter all Black almshouse inmates. The Colored Orphan Asylum's first building was on Fifth Avenue between Forty-Second and Forty-Third Streets but was burned to the ground during the 1863 draft riots and relocated to Harlem and later the Bronx.

14. Gunja SenGupta, *From Slavery to Poverty: The Racial Origins of Welfare in New York, 1840–1918* (New York: New York University Press, 2009), 11–13.

15. Following the 1863 destruction of the orphanage's first building, the New York Colored Orphan Asylum relocated to 143rd Street and Amsterdam Avenue, where they constructed a new building in 1867. Iver Bernstein, *The New York City Draft Riots: Their Significance for American Society and Politics in the Age of the Civil War* (New York: Oxford University Press, 1990), 27.

16. Alice Kessler-Harris, *Out to Work: A History of Wage-Earning Women in the United States* (New York: Oxford University Press, 1982), 90–92.

17. Nicola Sleapwood and Thomas D. Hamm, "Quakers and the Social Order, 1830–1937," in *The Creation of Modern Quaker Diversity, 1830–1937*, ed. Stephen W. Angell, Pink Dandelion, and David Harrington Watt (University Park: Pennsylvania University Press, 2023), 185–86.

18. *Annual Report of the New York Colored Mission* (New York, 1875), 4.

19. *Annual Report of the New York Colored Mission* (New York, 1885), 5; *Annual Report of the New York Colored Mission* (New York, 1892), 3.

20. "The Wages of Women," *The Current* 7, no. 166 (February 19, 1887): 241–42.

21. *Annual Report of the New York Colored Mission* (New York, 1901), 14.

22. Theda Skocpol, *Protecting Soldiers and Mothers: The Political Origins of Social Policy in the United States* (Cambridge, Mass.: Harvard University Press, 1992).

23. Timothy J. Gilfoyle, *City of Eros: New York City, Prostitution, and the Commercialization of Sex, 1790–1920* (New York: W.W. Norton, 1994), 209.

24. Ernest Albert Bell, *Fighting the Traffic in Young*

Girls: Or, War on the White Slave Trade (1910), 174–89; "A Review of the World," *Current Literature* 46 (1909): 594–98. See also Brian Donovan, *White Slave Crusades: Race, Gender, and Anti-Vice Activism, 1887–1917* (Champaign: University of Illinois Press, 2010), 89–109.

25. Genna Rae McNeil, Houston Bryan Roberson, Quinton Hosford Dixie, and Kevin McGruder, *Witness: Two Hundred Years of African-American Faith and Practice at the Abyssinian Baptist Church of Harlem, New York* (Grand Rapids, Mich.: William B. Eerdmans Publishing, 2013), 59.

26. "The Assaults on Negroes in New York," *Public Opinion* 29 (New York, 1900), 231.

27. Paul Laurence Dunbar, "Negroes of the Tenderloin," *The Sun* (New York), September 4, 1897.

28. Shelton H. Bishop, "A History of St. Philip's Church, New York City," *Historical Magazine of the Protestant Episcopal Church* 15, no. 4 (1946): 302.

29. Bishop, "A History of St. Philip's Church," 306–7.

30. Nancy Dickinson, "St. Philip's Episcopal Church Cemetery Intensive Documentary Study/Chrystie Street, New York, New York/Second Avenue Subway," prepared by Historical Perspectives, Inc. (Westport, Conn., June 2003), 13; "St. Philip's Church May Sell," *New York Age*, March 23, 1911. Nineteenth-century financial, racial, and administrative relationships between St. Philip's and Trinity were very complicated. Despite St. Philip's break from Trinity, they continued to be tied to their former congregation through Trinity's influence over the Episcopal diocese. For more, see John H. Hewitt Jr., *Protest and Progress: New York's First Black Episcopal Church Fights Racism* (New York: Garland Publishing, 2000).

31. The original address for the lot was 81 West Thirtieth Street but was changed to 127 at some point before 1872. Several Irish families are recorded as having lived at the address. See *New York Daily Herald,* July 16, 1859; *New York Daily Herald,* April 20, 1871.

32. Carla L. Peterson, *Black Gotham: A Family History of African Americans in Nineteenth-Century New York City* (New Haven, Conn.: Yale University Press, 2011), 338.

33. *Statistical Report of the Women in the State of New York* (Chicago: Columbian Exposition, 1893), 52, https://www.google.com/books/edition/Statistical_Report_of_the_Women_in_the_S/YLEyAQAAMAAJ?hl=en&gbpv=1.

34. For more on this architectural pattern as it pertains to Black old age homes, see Willa Granger, "Eldercare at the Margins: Keeping Up to Code at the Stephen Smith Home," *Pennsylvania Magazine of History and Biography* 145, no. 3 (October 2021): 305–38; Leslie J. Pollard, "Black Beneficial Societies and the Home for Aged and Infirm Colored Persons: A Research Note," *Phylon* 41, no. 3 (1980): 230–34; Susan C. Reed and Nancy Davis, "The Jane Dent Home: The Rise and Fall of Homes for the Aged in Low-Income Communities," *Journal of Health Care for the Poor and Underserved* 15, no. 4 (November 2004): 547–61.

35. "St. Philip's Parish House on Boston Road," *Bronx Times*, September 20–26, 2019.

36. *Building: An Architectural Monthly* 25, no. 11 (September 12, 1896): 123.

37. Richard Plunz, *A History of Housing in New York City*, rev. ed. (New York: Columbia University Press, 2016), 37; *Laws of the State of New York*, vol. 2 (New York State Legislative Bill Drafting Commission, 1882), 182; Glenn P. Crobett, "Fire Escapes," in *The Encyclopedia of New York City*, 2nd ed., ed. Kenneth T. Jackson, Lisa Keller, and Nancy Flood (New Haven, Conn.: Yale University Press, 2010), 448.

38. *United States Census, 1900,* New York County, ED 676 Borough of Manhattan, Election District 8–9 New York City Ward 25, image 16 of 42; citing National Archives and Records Administration (NARA) microfilm publication T623 (Washington, D.C.: National Archives and Records Administration). Database with images accessed via FamilySearch, https://familysearch.org/ark:/61903/3:1:S3HT-67X3-75G?cc=1325221&wc=9B77-441%3A1030551901%2C1035804001%2C1036127601 : 5 August 2014. Family Search is the genealogical website of the Church of Jesus Christ of Latter-day Saints. You must create a free account to access the site.

39. Tenants are reported to have hosted musical recitals and dances, organized benevolent associations, and more. See "Annual Clambake and Outing," *New York Age*, August 30, 1906; "Manhattan and the Bronx," *New York Age*, October 4, 1906; "Obituary: Mrs. Elizabeth Madocer," *New York Age*, December 13, 1906.

40. Marcy S. Sacks, *Before Harlem: The Black Experience in New York City before World War I* (Philadelphia: University of Pennsylvania Press, 2006), 180.

41. Elizabeth Blackmar, *Manhattan for Rent,*

1785–1850 (Ithaca, N.Y.: Cornell University Press, 1989), 250–53.

42. Felice Batlan, "Gender and the Rise of the Welfare State in Fin-de-Siècle New York City: The Case of Tenement Regulation," in *The Legal Tender of Gender: Welfare, Law and the Regulation of Women's Poverty,* ed. Shelley A. M. Gavigan and Dorothy E. Chunn (Oxford: Hart Publishing, 2010), 87–90.

43. *The American Florist* 11, no. 414 (May 9, 1896): 1106; *United States Census, 1900, New York,* New York County, ED 676 Borough of Manhattan, Election District 8–9 New York City Ward 25, image 16 of 42; citing NARA microfilm publication T623 (Washington, D.C.: National Archives and Records Administration). Database with images accessed via FamilySearch, https://familysearch.org/ark:/61903/3:1:S3HT-67X3 -75G?cc=1325221&wc=9B77-441%3A1030551901%2C 1035804001%2C1036127601 : 5 August 2014. Family Search is the genealogical website of the Church of Jesus Christ of Latter-day Saints. You must create a free account to access the site.

44. Kevin McGruder, *Race and Real Estate: Conflict and Cooperation in Harlem, 1890–1920* (New York: Columbia University Press, 2017), 105–6.

45. Hewitt, *Protest and Progress,* 135.

46. Quoted in Ralph E. Luker, *The Social Gospel in Black and White: American Racial Reform, 1885–1912* (Chapel Hill: University of North Carolina Press, 2000), 172.

47. Victoria Earle Matthews, "The Negroes of New York," *The Sun* (New York), September 13, 1897, 6.

48. *United States Census, 1900, New York,* New York County, ED 676 Borough of Manhattan, Election District 8–9 New York City Ward 25, image 16 of 42; citing NARA microfilm publication T623 (Washington, D.C.: National Archives and Records Administration, n.d.). Database with images, accessed via FamilySearch, https://familysearch.org/ark:/61903/3:1:S3HT-67X3 -75G?cc=1325221&wc=9B77-441%3A1030551901%2C 1035804001%2C1036127601 : 5 August 2014. Family Search is the genealogical website of the Church of Jesus Christ of Latter-day Saints. You must create a free account to access the site.

49. McGruder, *Race and Real Estate,* 98.

50. Quoted in Hilary Ballon, *New York's Pennsylvania Stations* (New York: W.W. Norton, 2002), 35.

51. Ballon, *New York's Pennsylvania Stations,* 37; Paul M. Kaplan, *New York's Original Penn Station: The*

Rise and Tragic Fall of an American Landmark (Charleston, S.C.: The History Press, 2019), 53.

52. Augustine E. Costello, *Our Police Protectors: History of the New York Police from the Earliest Period to the Present Time* (New York, 1884), 452.

53. Sacks, *Before Harlem,* 39–41.

54. "The Most Important Police Precinct in America," *New York Times,* May 1, 1904, 28; "Disease Lurks in Police Station Cells," *New-York Tribune,* May 28, 1905, 45. During the 1890s, approximately 2.5 percent of arrests were of Black people, which doubled to over 5 percent after 1900. As historian Marcy Sacks describes this development, "No other single group in the city experienced comparable levels of animosity from daily encounters with policemen." Marcy S. Sacks, "'Skull Trouble': A Brief History of Police Harassment of Black New Yorkers," Gotham Center for New York City History (website), April 23, 2020, https://www .gothamcenter.org/blog/skull-trouble-a-brief-history -of-police-harassment-of-black-new-yorkers.

55. "Lively Record of the Tenderloin, Which Wants a New Station House," *The Sun,* December 4, 1904, 16.

56. *Annual Report of the New York Colored Mission* (New York, 1901), 8.

57. "New York Colored Mission," *The Survey* 8, no. 3 (January 18, 1902): 67.

58. *New York Daily Herald,* February 28, 1856, 7.

59. *Real Estate Record and Builders' Guide* 67 (February 9, 1901): 238.

60. McAdoo, *Guarding a Great City,* 140.

61. "New Tenderloin Station," *New York Times,* June 7, 1905, 15.

62. "Mission Without a Home," *The Sun,* September 8, 1905, 12; "A Homeless Negro Church," *New York Times,* September 7, 1905, 7. Curiously, Reverend Wilson is listed as living at one of the properties owned by St. Philip's (117 West Thirtieth Street) in 1906. See *Directory of Social and Health Agencies of New York City* (New York: Charity Organization Society, 1906), 325.

63. McAdoo, *Guarding a Great City,* 141; "Old 'Tenderloin' Station Awaiting Its Doom,' *New York Times,* May 13, 1906, 34.

64. "Architectural Aberration—The Twenty-Third Precinct Police Station, New York," *Architectural Record* 30 (July–December 1911), 182.

65. William McAdoo, "Experiences of a Police Commissioner: IV. Problems of Crime and Detection," *Harper's Weekly* 50 (January 6, 1906): 741.

66. "Know Nothing Detectives," *The Sun,* June 8, 1899; "Tenderloin Robberies as Told by Moss Agents," *Brooklyn Daily Eagle,* August 9, 1899.

67. McAdoo, *Guarding a Great City,* 142.

68. "McAdoo Explains Race Riots," *New York Age,* July 20, 1905, 4.

69. Ballon, *New York's Pennsylvania Stations,* 33.

70. "Woman Official Familiar with Job on Her First Day," *The Evening World,* January 2, 1914, 2.

71. See Anya Jabour, "An 'Adamless Eden for Female Offenders'?: Katharine Bement Davis and the Carceral State in Progressive-Era New York," *Society for Historians of the Gilded Age and Progressive Era,* July 13, 2021, https://www.shgape.org/an-adamless-eden-for-female-offenders/.

72. Landmark Preservation Commission, *St. Philip's Protestant Episcopal Church* (Designation List 252 LP–1846) (New York: City of New York, 1993), 5; McGruder, *Race and Real Estate,* 103.

73. "Parish House Sold," *New York Age,* December 23, 1909, 2.

74. "Vertner Woodson Tandy," in *African American Architects: A Biographical Dictionary, 1865–1945,* ed. Dreck Spurlock Wilson (New York: Routledge, 2003), 543.

75. McGruder, *Race and Real Estate,* 81.

76. Cheryl L. Greenberg, *Or Does It Explode?: Black Harlem in the Great Depression* (New York: Oxford University Press, 1997), 40–41.

Reviews

Travis C. McDonald
Poplar Forest: Thomas Jefferson's Villa Retreat
Charlottesville: University of Virginia Press, 2023
xx + 322 pages, 101 black-and-white illustrations, 33 line drawings
ISBN: 9780813949635, HB $49.50
ISBN: 9780813949642 EB $49.50

Review by Clifton Ellis

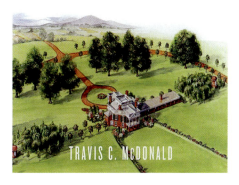

Travis McDonald, Director of Architectural Restoration of Poplar Forest, has spent the last thirty-four years conducting a meticulous restoration of Poplar Forest, Jefferson's private retreat in Bedford County, Virginia. McDonald considers it to be Jefferson's "most important and personal work of architecture" (xiii). McDonald's book recounts the remarkable story of Jefferson and Poplar Forest in clear, well-organized prose. McDonald takes a bewildering array of sources, including the minutiae of construction details, and weaves a story that is fascinating, informative, and never boring. He provides three appendices. Appendix A is a chronology of Jefferson's life and the construction of Poplar Forest. Appendix B is a list of helpful and interesting definitions of Jeffersonian elements and materials. Finally, Appendix C brings together for comparison and edification Jefferson's typology of octagon designs. McDonald's bibliography is evidence of thorough and well-sourced research, and the index is helpful to the reader. These are all the result of a long and thoughtful reflection on the project of restoring Poplar Forest and how that restoration reveals many facets of Thomas Jefferson, not the least of which is his development as an architect. The physical quality of the book leaves something to be desired; the uncoated paper stock does not allow for sharp images and drawings. A book of this nature in which illustrations are integral needs coated, glossy paper so that print, images, and drawings are sharp and crisp.

McDonald tells us that the best way to understand Jefferson as an architect is to study three sets of different but interrelated documents. The first set is the treasure trove of Jefferson papers held by the Coolidge family (now housed at the Massachusetts Historical Society). Fiske Kimball was the first historian to mine this source of more than seven hundred Jefferson drawings, ranging from plans, sections, and elevations, calculations of proportions, and drawings of construction materials and techniques. The drawings show a mind at work, experimenting with architectural details, working on the proportions and details of the classical orders, and designing ideal geometric forms that fascinated him, which eventually found their way into his design for Poplar Forest. Jefferson's Memorandum Books and his Farm Book are two documents that McDonald also considers important to understanding Jefferson the architect. These two sources, considered together, show Jefferson as a construction supervisor, detailing specifications for quantities of materials and working on perfecting an understanding of building processes and techniques. Finally, there is Jefferson's Building Notebook that contains more drawings and written specifications for every detail of a building project. For Monticello, no detail was too small. He specified doors and windows, chimney flues, architectural ornaments for entablatures, and wallpaper. These sources show that Jefferson had a keen awareness of space, light, and volume—further proof that Jefferson was thinking three dimensionally and holistically about his designs. These sources reveal the mind of an architect, just as other Jefferson sources reveal the mind of a politician or statesman.

Previous works on Jefferson's Poplar Forest were limited to a few articles and two academic theses until S. Allen Chambers Jr.'s *Poplar Forest and Thomas Jefferson*.[1] Chambers conducted extensive research in the many Jefferson archives around the country, aiding his main goal to explain the conception, construction, and use of the house. He also provided well-executed plans, elevations, cutaway perspectives, isometrics, and sections. Chambers gives good insights into Jefferson and his ideas of architecture.

For thirty years, Chambers's book was the definitive history of Poplar Forest. McDonald's book has the advantage over the Chambers book in two ways. First, McDonald has the benefit of directing to completion a thirty-year restoration of the building, and he knows every inch and detail of Poplar Forest in a way that Chambers, through no fault of his own, could not have known in 1993. Secondly, McDonald has more closely analyzed Jefferson in the context of his personal and public life, his education, and his self-taught understanding and mastery of architecture.

After Jefferson's death, Poplar Forest changed hands numerous times. It burned in 1845, leaving only a shell, and subsequent owners altered the building so that Jefferson's intent, design, and materials were destroyed. Except for its octagonal form, very little of Jefferson's original design could be discerned. In 1984 the nonprofit Corporation for Jefferson's Poplar Forest purchased the house and fifty acres, and in 1989 the herculean task of restoration began under the direction of McDonald. It lasted for thirty years.

Thomas Jefferson inherited the 4,819-acre estate and eleven enslaved men, women, and children in 1773 from his father-in-law, John Wayles, but Jefferson did little to improve the property before he began thinking of his retirement. McDonald explains to great effect Jefferson's need for solitude and how it influenced his plans for Poplar Forest. The classical literature that comprised Jefferson's education commended the Roman culture of villa retreats and retirement, and Jefferson relished the idea of a rural sanctuary surrounded by nature and cultivated fields, unsullied by the rude, boisterous, and corrupting influences of politics. In letters to friends and family, Jefferson often claimed that he preferred a simpler life at a retreat. These periods of solitude and intense concentration were constant throughout Jefferson's life. Jefferson had a lifelong need for periods of solitude during which he could read, write, and think uninterrupted.

Yet, Jefferson's was not a brooding solitude, rather, it was productive time alone. Jefferson told his daughter, Martha, that while still a boy and long before he built Monticello, he would go alone to the mountaintop when he wanted to read or think or marvel at the natural beauty that surrounded the little mountain. This desire for solitude stayed with Jefferson his entire life. While governor of Virginia, Jefferson would make journeys alone to his nearby Goochland County plantation and stay for days in the one-room brick house he kept there. While in Philadelphia, he rented a summer house outside the city where he spent days and weeks reading, writing, and corresponding without interruption. And his daughter Martha tells of Jefferson's frequent retirements to a place he called his hermitage on a hill overlooking Paris where he would work for a week or more on the business of his mission to France. These periods of solitude, concentration, and reflection were the reason for his stellar academic performance and achievements.

McDonald explains that understanding Jefferson's education is essential in understanding his design and construction at Poplar Forest. As Vitruvius advised in his first-century treatise, preparation as an architect should start first with a solid liberal arts education. Jefferson entered the College of William & Mary at Williamsburg in 1760 at age 16. His instructors, scholars of the classics who were steeped in the Scottish Enlightenment, described Jefferson as a precocious "hard student" with a "canine appetite" for reading who studied fifteen hours a day (35).[2] Although architecture was not part of the curriculum at William & Mary, it was an inherent interest of Jefferson's, and he bought as many books on architecture as he could. It is well known that Jefferson was an avid reader and that he constantly bought books from estate sales, from the publishers of the *Virginia Gazette,* from individuals, and from the booksellers in London. Through these books he learned theory and form.

Jefferson's book learning in architecture was accompanied by his very close observation of architecture everywhere he went. In Williamsburg and throughout Virginia his eye was trained in the Georgian Palladian style. He saw the best of new architecture in Annapolis, Philadelphia, New York, Boston, and Washington, D.C. While abroad he toured every significant site he could. Everywhere he went he talked to the carpenters, joiners, and masons at building sites, taking notes during these conversations on such things as materials, construction techniques, and time management.

In Appendix C of his book, McDonald re-produces thirty of Jefferson's plans and drawings in which Jefferson employs the octagon in a wide variety of combinations. Not all the plans are identified, but most are of plans for houses: three full octagonal plans; nine semi-octagonal bays; and eighteen plans with octagonal rooms. Jefferson also used the octagon for his design of the Anatomical Theater at the University of Virginia, and for unbuilt projects such as the observatory for the University of Virginia and a chapel in Williamsburg.

Jefferson clearly was fascinated with the octagon, the geometric shape that he used for Poplar Forest, and indeed, the octagon could be found in almost all the pattern books circulating during the eighteenth century. Certainly, Jefferson was aware of the shape's popularity, but he never explains why he preferred to use this form in so many of his designs. We have only an oblique reference to what might have been Jefferson's reasons for preferring the octagon. John Hartwell Cocke had asked Jefferson for plans to build a house at his plantation, Bremo, in Fluvanna County, Virginia, and those plans evidently included octagonal rooms. After seeing Jefferson's plan for Poplar Forest in 1816, Isaac Coles wrote to Cocke, "as you predicted he was for giving you Octagons. They gave you a semicircle of light and air. They were charming. He is a great advocate for light and air" (67). But Cocke rejected the novel forms and instead employed James Dinsmore, Jefferson's master builder for Monticello, to help design and build his house. These are the only hints we have for Jefferson's use of the octagon, but there must have been other reasons. We will never know for certain.

What is certain, as McDonald sees it, is Jefferson's unwavering adherence to Palladio. Jefferson told a friend that Palladio was "the bible. You should get it and stick close to it" (39). Palladio's sixteenth-century *Four Books of Architecture* focused largely on villa designs for the Venetian elite. McDonald goes on in detail to analyze the Palladian ratios and proportions that Jefferson meticulously followed at Poplar Forest. Palladio did allow for some adventure in molding details and entablature articulation, and Jefferson chose a simple version of Roman Doric and Tuscan orders and applied them to Poplar Forest and indeed most of his projects. Jefferson did take some liberties with entablature ornamentation, but he always justified diversions from Palladio. For Jefferson, Palladio was innovative, authoritative yet flexible, and importantly, a connection to the antique, which was crucial as lineage and precedent. English literature and the writings of the English landscape architects also informed Jefferson as he began to consider the design of his villa. It is in this context that McDonald makes an excellent and complete analysis of Jefferson's octagon and the ways in which he tried to make this geometry accommodate the functional aspects of a plantation household.

Jefferson's travels through England also influenced him, exposing him to the latest developments in English suburban villas and picturesque landscapes. His five-year diplomatic mission to Paris gave him the opportunity to study the advances in French neoclassicism and methods of construction as well as distinctly French architectural features such as room sequence. For example, in Paris, guests often went directly to table, following a sequence of entry vestibule, dining room, and drawing room, which is the sequence at Poplar Forest and one that was unlike any in America at the time. The skylight was a Parisian feature that Jefferson incorporated into his dining room at Poplar Forest. The French favored large paned windows reaching from the floor almost to the ceiling. Jefferson designed triple-sash windows that allowed one to pass from a room to a portico, thus diminishing the barrier between interior and exterior and allowing nature to be more readily experienced. Polished oak floors were another European aesthetic that he introduced. American floors were left untreated and did not have the oil and wax finish that brought a sheen and sense of finish to European floors. Both Monticello and Poplar Forest featured highly polished floors. Jefferson also incorporated inconspicuous stairways, jib doors, and hidden service de-

vices that he had in his rented house in Paris. Jefferson's unique synthesis of Palladio and Paris produced what is termed "Jeffersonian Classicism." Jefferson had an ability to synthesize influences, not merely copy them, and this ability is why Jefferson is an important figure in American architecture.

McDonald writes a fascinating and detailed chapter on the construction of Poplar Forest. Jefferson left Washington, D.C., in 1806 and headed to Poplar Forest, where he supervised the laying of the foundation of his private retreat. By 1809 the house was closed in, occupiable, and yet far from finished. Still, Jefferson began his retreats at Poplar Forest. In 1815, the walls, floors, and roof were complete and the interior of the house was ready for the carefully skilled John Hemings to begin work. Work continued over the next seventeen years, right up to Jefferson's death in 1826.

The workforce at both Monticello and Poplar Forest included free and enslaved workers. Jefferson had begun an apprenticeship program for some of his slaves at Monticello, having them taught nail making and brick and mortar making, among other useful building skills. One of his most reliable and trusted slaves was John Hemings, the brother of Sally Hemings. John Hemings had been well trained by Jefferson's British and Irish joiners, and Hemings became a professional himself. Jefferson gave Hemings his own set of tools and paid him twenty dollars a year to work at both Monticello and Poplar Forest. Hemings learned the rules and language of classical architecture, and he regularly corresponded knowledgeably with Jefferson about the work at Poplar Forest.

Hemings had three enslaved workers under his supervision—his nephews Beverly, Madison, and Eston—all sons of Jefferson and Sally Hemings. They were Jefferson's "shadow family" (171). They were the craftsmen who executed every classical detail at Poplar Forest to exact specifications, and their part in the construction of Jefferson's retreat is one of its most extraordinary aspects. Although they worked in close proximity with Jefferson from

1815 to 1826, there is little information about their relationship. In written records, they are referred to as "aids" to their uncle, and they are listed among the enslaved workers that Jefferson owned. There is a reference to buying cabbages from them, and there is a note that Eston once drove a cart to Poplar Forest.

In his will, Jefferson arranged the freedom of his unacknowledged shadow family. Beverly did not wait for his manumission, however. He simply walked away from his life of bondage in 1822. No attempt was made to recover him, which was very unusual for the time, and he disappeared from any historical record. Jefferson's will freed John Hemings, and although he did not immediately free Madison and Eston, he gave Hemings custody of his sons until they turned twenty-one, at which time they were to be freed. Madison moved to Ohio; he identified with the Black community, discussing his parentage in an 1873 newspaper article. Eston moved to Wisconsin, where he passed as White and never mentioned his family connections. Jefferson's biracial children and their descendants would not be officially recognized by the Thomas Jefferson Foundation until 1998, when DNA results proved the link.

McDonald writes, "The goal of good architectural restoration then, given the variable circumstances of each site, is to present an authentic historical 'fact' based on objective research and analysis" (213). The goal of this long restoration project was to know more about Thomas Jefferson through understanding the most intimate spaces he designed for himself. The restoration enriches our understanding of Jefferson's architectural works. Analyzing the construction of the house reveals the role that Jefferson's enslaved workers played in fulfilling his vision even as it raises more questions about his relationship with his biracial sons and Jefferson's own role as an enslaver. McDonald acknowledges that the historical facts discovered through objective research and analysis are open to many interpretations from many different perspectives, and he does not try to shape the reader's perceptions. Rather, both his restoration of Poplar Forest and his book are offered up as two more sources to consider as we grapple with the legacy of the elusive Thomas Jefferson.

AUTHOR BIOGRAPHY

Clifton Ellis earned his PhD in Architectural History at the University of Virginia with a focus on antebellum plantation landscapes. He is Elizabeth Sasser Professor of Architectural History and Associate Dean of Research at Texas Tech University's College of Architecture.

NOTES

1. S. Allen Chambers Jr., *Poplar Forest & Thomas Jefferson* (Forest, Va.: The Corporation for Jefferson's Poplar Forest, 1993).

2. McDonald quotes Merrill Peterson, ed., *Thomas Jefferson: Writings,* Library of America 17 (New York: Literary Classics of the United States, 1984), 12.

Dale W. Tomich,
Rafael de Bivar Marquese,
Reinaldo Funes Monzote,
Carlos Venegas Fornias

Reconstructing the Landscapes of Slavery: A Visual History of the Plantation in the Nineteenth-Century Atlantic World

Chapel Hill: University of North Carolina Press, 2021
176 pages, 84 color plates, 1 map, 1 table
ISBN: 9781469663128, PB $29.95
ISBN: 9781469663111, HB $95.00
ISBN: 9781469663135, EB $24.99

Review by Asiel Sepúlveda[1]

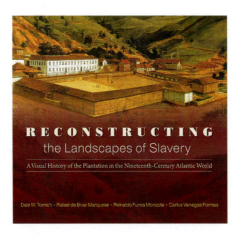

For centuries, the American[2] plantation has been the subject of fascination and study. Such interests can be traced to Dennis Diderot's *Encyclopédie* (1762–72), where a Caribbean sugar state is carefully described in text and image.[3] Today, the plantation, as place and concept, continues to fuel scholarly debate. While the socioeconomic history of these enterprises is well documented, scholars are seeking greener pastures in an extensive visual record that, until recently, sat undisturbed in the pages of history books. The volume *Reconstructing the Landscapes of Slavery: A Visual History of the Plantation in the Nineteenth-Century Atlantic World* promises to utilize these sources for a closer look at the nineteenth-century plantation. Written by historians from Cuba, Brazil, and the United States, the book transports us into the now faded landscapes of slavery in the Western Hemisphere. The authors concentrate on archives of visual culture—maps, lithographs, photographs, technical drawings, and other images—that help us "reconstruct" said landscapes. But can we truly reconstruct historic spaces via their representations? Are these images trustworthy given the power structures that produced them?

In the introduction to the volume, the authors Dale W. Tomich, Rafael de Bivar Marquese, Reinaldo Funes Monzote, and Carlos Venegas Fornias discuss the complications of utilizing the image as a historic document. They reflect on interpretive methods employed by art historians, who consider the image as a cultural and discursive object that transacts in a world of aesthetics. Art historians, the authors tell us, have deemed the landscape a "way of seeing," a way of organizing space in a visual and symbolic plane where the master projects his power over the land and his subjects. The authors insist that it is not enough to read these power structures in the images; the landscape should not be reduced to its formal representations, they tell us. Instead, they propose an examination of the material conditions of a place that is built, lived, and viewed from various perspectives. Such understanding is theorized using the concept of "working landscapes" defined as "the continual interplay of material conditions, forms of social relations of slavery, and historically shaped meanings and modes of symbolic expression" (9). The emphasis is not on the image itself, but rather on the relations that it represents. Thus, the authors attempt to mine the "documentary character" of the image (10).

Following the introduction, a second introductory text opens the historical analysis. Here, the authors anchor their studies on the conceptual framework of the "second slavery." Proposed by Tomich over a decade ago, the second slavery describes the nineteenth-century expansion and redeployment of African bonded laborers into new economic frontiers of the southern United States, western Cuba, and southeastern Brazil. In these renewed geographies of slavery, coerced labor was restructured and adapted in combination with emergent industrial technologies optimized to cultivate a single cash crop—cotton, sugar, or coffee—on a mass scale. This phenomenon, Tomich explains, is a type of second slavery whose new forms responded to the advent of industrialization and a growing consumer culture in the Western world.

Reconstructing the Landscapes of Slavery thus centers on the geographies of the second slavery in the United States, Cuba, and Brazil. The book is divided into two parts. The first offers a historical overview of each "commodity frontier." The second provides an in-depth analysis of its spaces, ecologies, and modes of production. In each section we read chapters dedicated to a single region and not to the intersections between them. This is not to say that the chapters appear disconnected from each other. To the contrary, the reader will effortlessly connect the structures and practices that unite the landscapes of the second slavery.

The authors provide a stimulating discussion about the spatial economy of the plantation. They explain, in great detail, the characteristics of cash crops, and how each demanded different uses of the land, industrial technologies, and enslaved labor. For example, cotton plantations in the Mississippi Valley found economic efficiency with semi-mechanized systems and one hundred enslaved workers. On the other hand, the Cuban and Brazilian sugar and coffee estates housed over three hundred slaves alongside highly mechanized production facilities. Given the new desire to surveil and control large numbers of enslaved Africans, planters abandoned the *bohíos* in Cuba and the *casas de sapé* in Brazil, both small, thatched-roof dwellings that housed enslaved families. Instead, they built barracoons, or large rectangular buildings with a single entrance that shared the architectural language of prisons built in the early nineteenth century. This is one of the many changes that illustrate how the nineteenth-century plantation modified the space and life of its inhabitants.

The volume invites readings that interlace the different geographies of slavery. It is here where we find the principal contribution of the book. We must applaud the authors' historical acumen and their ability to synthetize and present the three regions on a relational plane. The carefully crafted discussion provides visual and material testimony to the second slavery, a concept that previously existed in abstracted theory and macroeconomic figures. The authors successfully present the landscapes of slavery as spaces that are calculated, constructed, and modified by the impulses of industrial modernity and the cultures of consumption that they generated. It is clear that the plantation was not a belated place of nineteenth-century modernity, but an integral part of it. Such modernity is also present in the visual culture studied. The images presented not only document the modification of the

landscape and the technological innovations of each region, but they show themselves as ambassadors of such modernity.

Reconstructing the Landscapes of Slavery delivers on its promises to investigate the "working landscapes" of the plantation, but it lacks a critical engagement with the visual culture it studies. On multiple occasions the chapters maintain a narrative thread in which the image illustrates an already established argument. It is not clear whether the image is the main source of analysis, a departing point, or needed at all. The reader will find it difficult to locate themselves in the reproduced maps given that authors dedicate little time to explain them, and the text or keys within these maps, particularly those of the Mississippi Valley, are illegible. If we cannot position ourselves on the map or read its keys, then these images function like an abstract painting: lines, rectangles, circles, and squares divide the space into grids and plains of color. What does this abstraction say about the plantation and its modernity? The reader who comes to the text with a certain curiosity for the visual logic of the plantation will find abundant stimulus in the images but not in the analysis. Visual culture appears here as a bridge to a material reality—a bridge that might be full of holes and illusions. The search for historical materiality has blinded the authors to the manipulations of the image. Thus, the cleanliness and spotless machinery of a sugar factory that burns spent sugarcane all day are not questioned; neither is the representation of idle slaves marveling at the grandiosity of industrial machinery, nor the poses of enslaved workers and overseers spread around a coffee field and clearly arranged by the photographer to create a "natural" image of slavery. The authors present the pictures as sources that document a reality, but I see images constructing one.

Methodologically, *Reconstructing the Landscapes of Slavery* presents an important step toward an interdisciplinary approach to plantation studies where methods from history, art history, and visual culture are considered

and negotiated. However, the book and this review, written by an art historian, show how disciplinary interests continue to shape our inquiries. Regardless of one's disciplinary disposition, the investigation must be applauded for revealing the nineteenth-century plantation, its techniques of measuring and organizing the land, and its implementation of new processes of production and accounting. We also learn about the extensive biological manipulation of crops and the land itself, and how the ecological environment shaped regimes of work and slavery. Moreover, the authors successfully present parallel historical analysis, fusing a hemispheric perspective to the study of nineteenth-century slave societies.

The volume is an admirable attempt at "reconstructing" plantation landscapes. However, it overlooks a major line of inquiry: the lives of the enslaved. The forced workers appear frequently in the text and images, yet we learn very little about them. Who were they? How did the new systems of the second slavery affect the formation of slave communities? These questions arise in the fourth chapter in which we see images of worship and dancing on a cotton plantation. While the authors mention the presence of a "human community," they quickly return to the strenuous work regimen and techniques of exploitation on the plantation. Therefore, the reader finds it difficult to disassociate the enslaved from their inhumane labor. A historic reconstruction of the plantation demands a closer view of the lives, intimacies, and cultures of those who inhabited the landscapes of nineteenth-century slavery.

Reconstructing the Landscapes of Slavery offers an important contribution to the understanding of a past so complex that it escapes the margins of a single study. It is a valuable resource for those interested in the particularities and multipolarity of nineteenth-century slavery. The book introduces us to a rich visual archive that documented and shaped the world of the plantation. In turn, it invites us to look more closely and critically into the image of slavery.

AUTHOR BIOGRAPHY

Asiel Sepúlveda is Assistant Professor of Art History and Visual Culture at Babson College. His research examines the development of lithographic arts in colonial Cuba, and its role in shaping imaginaries of Caribbean cosmopolitanism. Sepúlveda received a PhD in Art History from the Rhetorics of Art, Space and Culture Program at Southern Methodist University, and a B.A. from Florida International University.

NOTES

1. The review of this book was originally published in Spanish in the journal *Perspectivas Afro* 1, vol. 2 (Julio–Diciembre 2022), https://doi.org/10.32997/pa-2022. Its publication in English has been authorized by the journal's editors.

2. I use "American" to refer to the broader continental Americas.

3. Dennis Diderot and Jean L. Alembert, *Encyclopédie, ou Dictionnaire raisonné des sciences, des arts et métiers* (Paris: Braisson [etc.], 1762–72), leaf 43.

David Monteyne
For the Temporary Accommodation of Settlers: Architecture and Immigrant Reception in Canada, 1870–1930
Montreal: McGill-Queen's University Press, 2021
344 pages, 126 photos
ISBN: 9780228006381, HB $75.00
ISBN: 9780228007555, EB $60.00

Review by Catherine Boland Erkkila

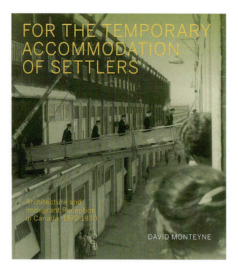

A country's borders, an often-overlooked physical space in which people are either admitted or denied entry, contain a wealth of cultural information. Within the field of architectural history, however, immigration architecture—reception facilities, quarantine hospitals, and detention stations—has yet to be fully explored. The design of these spaces and the experience of its occupants can reveal much about a country's governmental policies and cultural milieu. In this richly illustrated and beautifully designed volume, David Monteyne provides a comprehensive analysis of Canada's immigration architecture built from 1870 to the mid-1930s and the spatial practices it shaped. Canada's Dominion government facilitated entry and provided accommodations for the "desirable" (European) immigrants, while also establishing carceral spaces for the "undesirable" immigrants, defined by race, unemployment, poverty, poor health, or political orientation.

To explore this history, Monteyne employs a two-pronged approach: first, analysis and interpretation of archival documents, including architectural plans, official correspondence, and policy statements; and, second, the voices of the immigrants themselves as told through a variety of first-person sources such as memoirs and letters. This methodology provides a comprehensive understanding of Canada's immigration architecture from the formal strategies of government design, intent, and oversight to the informal spatial practices of the individual or group, influenced by what Henri Lefebvre calls the "lived experience." In short, the book addresses these questions: what were the intentions of the Canadian government in establishing these immigrant reception buildings, and how did migrants use these spaces? With thoughtfulness and theoretical rigor, Monteyne reveals the answers to these questions and provides ample visual evidence to support his thesis.

Monteyne's interpretation of this visual evidence is one of the greatest strengths of this book. Using floor plans, elevations, architectural detail drawings, and historic photographs, Monteyne deftly interprets the purpose of these structures, the intent behind their construction, and how these buildings were actually used. Monteyne makes excellent use of these many archival documents and enhances his own analysis with the immigrants' own voices. The book is organized chronologically and typographically, with each chapter dedicated to a specific building type or typological grouping of structures: pier buildings, quarantine stations, Prairie immigration halls in Canada's western provinces, and detention hospitals. The first three chapters explore structures built from the Confederation to the early twentieth century; the final two chapters span the early twentieth century to the mid-1930s. As thoroughly illustrated in each chapter, the spatial arrangements of these buildings changed over time in response to Canadian immigration policies. For example, with the introduction of medical and civil inspections, the architectural program of pier buildings in particular became more complex to accommodate new functions. Likewise, the design of detention facilities changed due to stakeholder input and the detained immigrants' behavior. Monteyne reveals how the immigrants' resistance to detention is in fact an example of how "global politics of quarantine played out as a local negotiation of spatial practices" (87).

What is most striking about Canada's immigration policies is that the government prioritized an immigration infrastructure throughout the entire country. The fundamental motivation behind this network, Monteyne notes, was the state's consistent paternalistic protection and provision of supportive institutions to welcome immigrants. This makes the immigrant experience in Canada quite unique. In the United States, by contrast, federal immigration infrastructure was focused on the large port cities (the most famous, of course, being Ellis Island in New York), while immigrants traveling farther into America's interior were left to the mercy of the private transportation companies, some of whom offered free tickets for those who purchased land (called "land explorer" passes) and occasionally temporary lodging. In Canada, however, the government immigration infrastructure was not isolated to the ports but extended into the Prairie settlements, with reception halls and social services established to assist newcomers. The Dominion government intended for this immigration network to distinguish Canada on the global stage as an attractive destination, particularly in contrast to the United States. Monteyne demonstrates how this systemization of immigrant reception was influenced by the concurrent modernization undertaken by public and private institutions at the turn of the twentieth century. And, for European immigrants at least, this system was largely beneficial.

The chapter on quarantine stations is especially timely, and provides a historical context for quarantine procedures and fumigation techniques. Monteyne reveals that Canada's quarantine facilities were largely an "architecture of panic," built to respond to present crises or future situations but never quite able to fulfill their intended purpose. Furthermore, race and class often determined one's experience of quarantine—an unfortunate fact that was also the case in the United States. These facilities were, Monteyne notes, important "stages for the performance of border surveillance" (90). Here, Monteyne addresses one of the most important points in the study of immigration architecture: public perception of these facilities was often just as significant as the architecture itself. This is particularly evident on the west coast, where Asian immigrants were often treated worse than European steerage passengers on the east coast (this anti-Asian sentiment was even more pervasive in the United States). At William Head, for example, the Dominion government erected a quarantine station in 1893 that

was heralded in the local news as a first-rate facility where "no germ or microbe" could survive (69). Quelling the public's fear of contagious disease was important, although the station itself was riddled with material and design deficiencies that rendered the facility ineffective. And yet, those inconsistencies did not matter to the public—the mere presence of the facility was comfort enough. Indeed, the superintendent asserted that that station would play an integral role in protecting the public from diseases from "the Orient" (69).

The hierarchy of immigrants parallels the experience in the United States, with both governments perceiving northern Europeans as the most desirable immigrants suitable to the various agricultural pursuits needed to support the nation. These migrants were courted by both Canada and the United States for agriculture and other specific labor needs. Unlike the United States, where immigrants were largely on their own after entry into the country, the social welfare programs the Dominion government offered during an immigrant's first year or two in the country was certainly appealing to Europeans and to Midwestern Americans, whom Canada also pursued. The Prairie immigration halls, where potential homesteaders could stay for free for days or weeks, were a critical lifeline for many immigrants and for Canadian settlers during the harsh winter months. Yet even in these buildings the hierarchy persisted, with British citizens separated from other European immigrants. Ultimately, it was the continued growth of welfare-state supports that contributed to the demise of Canada's immigration infrastructure. The buildings were rendered obsolete and many were demolished as cities and towns continued to develop.

Prairie immigration halls, while perhaps not architecturally distinct, played a significant role in town development. Monteyne describes how they evolved from their original use to become community sites for social events, entertainment, or judicial purposes. A close reading of their floorplans then becomes critical in understanding how these

buildings and rooms actually functioned, which Monteyne does with aplomb. Monteyne also includes descriptions of furnishings, signage, and other elements of material culture to further his argument. Like the architectural plans and designs, these items reinforced the systemization of Canada's immigration network and are significant elements in any analysis of immigration architecture. Government regulations concerning occupant behaviors in immigration halls were posted throughout the buildings to educate newcomers on the expected Canadian norms of behavior. Signs indicating where clothing should be washed and hung, for example, reinforced separation of space by function and are interpreted by Monteyne as corrective behaviors to a peasant class who might be more accustomed to single- or double-room houses. Furthermore, government efforts at reinforcing cleanliness addressed public fears of immigrants as dirty or diseased—a notion that is revealed in the quarantine stations and detention hospitals as well.

Amidst the analysis of these facilities, Monteyne includes firsthand accounts of the buildings and its services. The architecture forms an important backdrop for the lived experience of the immigrants occupying these spaces. The vast breadth of sources and voices of bureaucratic officials and migrants alike is woven together in engaging prose. As Monteyne skillfully reveals, it is through its immigration architecture that the government imparted its vision of Canadian society, one replete with racial and domestic hierarchies. Though few of these buildings are extant, with his research Monteyne has cemented them in Canadian architectural history. This book is a pivotal text for the study of immigration through a spatial lens and opens the door for further research, particularly the role of nongovernmental actors in the Canadian immigration network. Transportation companies, for example, were crucial in the development of a Canadian immigration network and establishing Prairie settlements on Indigenous lands. While purposefully

REVIEWS | **81**

excluded from this book in order to focus on the government's role, research into these nongovernmental actors would complement this robust volume.

This book offers a significant contribution to the fields of vernacular architecture and immigration studies, and provides a model for future research into immigration architecture. As Monteyne points out in his epilogue, historical analysis of immigration architecture has the potential to inform the contemporary design of immigrant reception and detention. It is worthwhile to consider these historical precedents when looking at the spatial dynamics of immigration in our current world. Race and class have always been determining factors in one's treatment during the migration process. The supportive network that Canada developed for its European immigrants, however, provides an impressive model from which much can be gleaned in terms of a humane approach to accommodating *all* migrants.

AUTHOR BIOGRAPHY

Catherine Boland Erkkila is managing editor of *SAH Archipedia* and the Buildings of the United States series, published by the Society of Architectural Historians and University of Virginia Press. Her book, *Spaces of Immigration: American Ports, Railways, and Settlements*, is forthcoming with the University of Pittsburgh Press.

Wei Zhao

Home beyond the House: Transformation of Life, Place, and Tradition in Rural China

Oxfordshire: Routledge, 2022

350 pages, 138 back-and-white illustrations

ISBN: 9781032280158, HB $160.00

ISBN: 9781003294948, EB $47.65

Review by Jing Xie

The urbanization process in China since the 1990s has brought fundamental changes to both urban and rural landscapes. According to the official statistics of China, the urbanization completion rate hit a record high of 65.22 percent in 2022.[1] As a result, cities have to be expanded vertically to accommodate more than half of China's population, many of whom migrated from rural areas. This seems to refute Fei Xiaotong's conclusion that "Chinese society is fundamentally rural," drawn from his extensive fieldwork in the early twentieth century.[2]

In parallel with development in cities, there have been several governmental campaigns and policies enacted with the aim of improving living conditions and the physical environment of Chinese villages. Yet without a profound understanding of rural culture, the attempt to revitalize villages seems to be somewhat fruitless under the overwhelming urbanization process. Traditional life is facing challenges with the transformation that is often portrayed by the media as a great revolution in China.

In this social context, Wei Zhao's *Home beyond the House: Transformation of Life, Place, and Tradition in Rural China* attempts to answer a simple question: "What constitutes the meaning of home for people living in traditional settlements in rural China?" (2). The book serves as a timely publication that critically assesses this widely acknowledged transformation. More remarkable is the drastic transformation of housing from the tradi-

tional or old to modern or new, changes that are often regarded as being synonymous with a *better* home. Zhao has tried to define the notion of home for the people living in vernacular settlements in rural China from physical, psychological, and social perspectives.

The book is well structured and presents research findings with rigor and clear logic. The theoretical framework is set up in the introduction. In particular, the meanings of "place," "home," "tradition," and "heritage" are introduced through citing the works of many preeminent scholars such as Amos Rapoport, Yi-Fu Tuan, Tim Cresswell, Edward Casey, David Harvey, Ronald Knapp, Fei Xiaotong, and David Lowenthal. Indeed, providing a long list of scholarly names seems to be a common feature when transforming PhD dissertations into books. Zhao similarly seems to be reluctant to curtail the literature review here, impairing the coherence of her key argument.

To better understand these concepts in context, chapter 1 offers a general history of the development of Chinese villages from 1949 to the present time. The changing policy on rural land ownership has had a fundamental influence on people's attachment to place.

There are also changes to family structure, population flow from rural to urban, and attitudes toward cultural traditions. All these have significantly shaped rural residents' lives and their home environments.

Chapter 2 starts by portraying the natural and cultural landscape of Yongkang County, where the case study, Yanxia Village, is located. The earliest settlement of the village in its form under the Cheng family can be traced back to the fourteenth century. The development of Yanxia Village is vividly presented through the historic narrative and an analysis of the physical structures, demonstrating the intertwined forces of family, society, and culture shaping the built environment. Chapter 3 continues the theme by exploring the local cultural landscape, focusing on traditions in classical learning and the worship of the local deity Hugong Dadi as historical background. This chapter goes on to discuss the cultural and local hospitality industry at the scale of individual buildings. As a culturally rooted practice, local family hotels contributed greatly to the cultural landscape of the village. These small businesses, however, are facing demolition during the government campaign of promoting and constructing local heritage with the aim of gaining recognition for Yanxia Village at national and international levels. This, perhaps, reflects a common phenomenon that heritage values are often misperceived by many local authorities in China.

Chapter 4 discusses the place-bound relationship reflected in the local lifestyle. As in many rural areas, Yanxia villagers are living self-sufficiently and are strongly attached to the place where their daily production, consumption, and recreation is rooted. Such an attachment has cultivated a sense of ownership that is beyond legal and material possession. Chapter 5 investigates how the notion of home is understood by the villagers through the case study of the Cheng family. The perceptions of home, as the author argues, are influenced by family history, lineage structure, and kinship. In particular, respect toward dis-

tant ancestors, pride in family achievements, and cohesion between the Cheng lineage and the vernacular environment have contributed to the understanding of home. Through daily practice, the trajectories of the individuals extend beyond their residential spaces to include public places and buildings, such as ancestral halls. Accordingly, their perceptions of home have expanded in physical and notional scope.

Economic standing is a dominant factor in leveraging family relationships. Linking back to chapter 4, chapter 6 adds an economic dimension to the understanding of home, as a household is a basic economic unit. Family-based economic practice emerged in Yanxia in the 1850s, serving the pilgrims of Hugong Dadi, and since then it has continuously shaped the cultural landscape of the village. As the business grew and the family multiplied, the competition and financial conflicts between family members also inevitably rose. On the other hand, those committed to the hospitality business missed many opportunities to be with their close family members during public holidays. This led to a detachment between families and individuals who were involved in the hospitality industry. As my own research on the mixed-use housing forms in medieval China illustrates, business was intertwined with daily life, thereby strengthening the family ties of the household.[3] This familial detachment in the modern era is a different yet interesting finding, perhaps due to the longtime development of individualism in China. As the author asserts, such economic practice "often led to detached and distant families and homes, and created residential spaces that were unable to protect privacy and support self-expression" (236).

In modern society, people may be less attached to their native places than they were previously. As a result of the urbanization process in China, there is a large rural population which has migrated into cities, and a person's residence is often remote from his or her place of origin. Chapter 7 examines the ways in which the embedded idea of *jiaxiang*

(native place) facilitates the meanings of home as understood by younger generations who moved away from their *jiaxiang*. Interestingly, no matter how far apart they are spatially, most young people are keen to recognize their family roots; they are emotionally attached to their *jiaxiang*.

Apart from summarizing the research outcomes, chapter 8 urges the reader to ponder the notion of "tradition" based on the fact that the once-lively Yanxia Village was eventually erased from the map in 2018 after most of the residents moved out, eleven years after the local government first announced the relocation plan in 2007. Yet a set of values in the form of traditions can withstand changes. This is evident under the striking changes across rural China brought forward by the movement connected with the Chinese Communist Party's "building a new socialist countryside" plan since 2006, in which the notion of home remains largely unchanged, maintaining long embedded values. Similarly, considering the recent urbanization process, the notion of home upheld by the new urbanites perhaps will not be much different to that felt by the younger generations of Yanxia villagers. To this end, Fei Xiaotong's claim that "Chinese society is fundamentally rural" still seems to be valid today. Yet villages, as the last stronghold of traditional life and form more or less preserved, are either dramatically disappearing or being transformed.

This book is based on the author's extended ethnographic fieldwork conducted between 2007 and 2019. Other than traditional research methodologies such as site survey, archival study, and interviews, a photovoice study was employed through distributing thirty-two single-use cameras to twenty-three residents and asking them to take photographs of meaningful aspects of their home. This is especially helpful for those villagers who are often unable to express their views and affections fully through words. The research is original, multidisciplinary, and comprehensive. Referring to the theoretical foundation discussed in the introduction, the research leaves room for more ambitious reach in challenging some of the theories imposed by those preeminent scholars. Perhaps it would be advantageous to articulate the theoretical contribution of this research more emphatically in chapter 8, instead of acquiescing with those scholars through simple summaries with citations.

There are many books on contemporary rural China, mostly focused on policy, economy, and sustainable development. In comparison with those works, Wei Zhao's approach from the architectural humanities is penetrating and refreshing. The book critically situates a modern-day transformation into a long historical context, through which the readers can gain a better grasp of the meanings of home in rural China. To those who are involved in the policy and movement of rural revitalization in China, this book will serve as an excellent guide.

AUTHOR BIOGRAPHY

Dr. Jing Xie is an architectural historian with research interests in the architecture and urbanism of China. He is the author of *The Origin and Development of Dougong and Zaojing in Early China* (2023), *Chinese Urbanism: Urban Form and Life in the Tang–Song Dynasties* (2020), and *Heritage-Led Urban Regeneration in China* (2017).

NOTES

1. National Bureau of Statistics of China, "Degree of Urbanization in China from 1980 to 2022," graph, January 17, 2023, https://www.statista.com/statistics/270162/urbanization-in-china/?crmtag=adwords&gclid=EAIaIQobChMIuf3Ihruj_wIV05jCCh2tWg1bEAAYASAAEgIG1vD_BwE&kw=.

2. Fei Xiaotong, *From the Soil: The Foundations of Chinese Society* (Berkeley: University of California Press, 1992), 37.

3. Jing Xie, *Chinese Urbanism: Urban Form and Life in the Tang–Song Dynasties* (Singapore: World Scientific, 2020), 84–86.

List of Editors: *Perspectives in Vernacular Architecture* and *Buildings & Landscapes*

Perspectives in Vernacular Architecture (1982); *Perspectives in Vernacular Architecture, II* (1986)

> EDITOR: Camille Wells

Perspectives in Vernacular Architecture, III (1989); *Perspectives in Vernacular Architecture, IV* (1991)

> EDITORS: Thomas Carter and Bernard L. Herman

Gender, Class, and Shelter: Perspectives in Vernacular Architecture, V (1995); *Shaping Communities: Perspectives in Vernacular Architecture, VI* (1997)

> EDITORS: Elizabeth Collins Cromley and Carter L. Hudgins

Exploring Everyday Landscapes: Perspectives in Vernacular Architecture, VII (1997); *People, Power, Places: Perspectives in Vernacular Architecture, VIII* (2000)

> EDITORS: Annmarie Adams and Sally McMurry

Constructing Image, Identity, and Place: Perspectives in Vernacular Architecture, IX (2003); *Building Environments: Perspectives in Vernacular Architecture, X* (2005)

> EDITORS: Alison K. Hoagland and Kenneth A. Breisch

Perspectives in Vernacular Architecture: The Journal of the Vernacular Architecture Forum 11 (2004); *Perspectives in Vernacular Architecture: The Journal of the Vernacular Architecture Forum* 12 (2005); *Perspectives in Vernacular Architecture: The Journal of the Vernacular Architecture Forum* 13.1 (2006)

> EDITORS: Jan Jennings and Pamela Simpson

Perspectives in Vernacular Architecture: The Journal of the Vernacular Architecture Forum 13.2 (2006/2007), Special 25th Anniversary Issue

> EDITORS: Warren Hofstra and Camille Wells

Buildings & Landscapes: Journal of the Vernacular Architecture Forum 14 (Fall 2007); 15 (Fall 2008); 16.1 (Spring 2009); 16.2 (Fall 2009)

> EDITORS: Howard Davis and Louis P. Nelson
> REVIEW EDITOR: Marilyn Castro

Buildings & Landscapes: Journal of the Vernacular Architecture Forum 17.1 (Spring 2010); 17.2 (Fall 2010); 18.1 (Spring 2011); 18.2 (Fall 2011); 19.1 (Spring 2012); 19.2 (Fall 2012)

> EDITORS: Marta Gutman and Louis P. Nelson
> REVIEW EDITOR: Andrew K. Sandoval-Strausz

Buildings & Landscapes: Journal of the Vernacular Architecture Forum 20.1 (Spring 2013); 20.2 (Fall 2013); 21.1 (Spring 2014); 21.2 (Fall 2014); 22.1 (Spring 2015); 22.2 (Fall 2015)

> EDITORS: Cynthia G. Falk and Marta Gutman
> REVIEW EDITOR: Andrew K. Sandoval-Strausz

Buildings & Landscapes: Journal of the Vernacular Architecture Forum 23.1 (Spring 2016); 23.2 (Fall 2016); 24.1 (Spring 2017); 24.2 (Fall 2017)

> EDITORS: Anna Vemer Andrzejewski and Cynthia G. Falk
> REVIEW EDITOR: Matthew Lasner

Buildings & Landscapes: Journal of the Vernacular Architecture Forum 25.1 (Spring 2018); 25.2 (Fall 2018); 26.1 (Spring 2019); 26.2 (Fall 2019)

> EDITORS: Anna Vemer Andrzejewski and Carl Lounsbury
> REVIEW EDITORS: Andrew Johnston and Jessica Ellen Sewell

Buildings & Landscapes: Journal of the Vernacular Architecture Forum 27.1 (Spring 2020); 27.2, Environmental Issue, Michael J. Chiarappa, Guest Editor (Fall 2020)

> EDITORS: Lydia Mattice Brandt and Carl Lounsbury
> REVIEW EDITORS: Andrew Johnston and Jessica Ellen Sewell

Buildings & Landscapes: Journal of the Vernacular Architecture Forum 28.1 (Spring 2021)

> EDITORS: Lydia Mattice Brandt and Carl Lounsbury
> EDITOR DESIGNATE: Michael J. Chiarappa
> REVIEW EDITORS: Andrew Johnston and Jessica Ellen Sewell

Buildings & Landscapes: Journal of the Vernacular Architecture Forum 28.2 (Fall 2021)

    EDITORS: Lydia Mattice Brandt and Carl Lounsbury
    EDITOR DESIGNATE: Michael J. Chiarappa
    REVIEW EDITOR: Rachel Leibowitz

Buildings & Landscapes: Journal of the Vernacular Architecture Forum 29.1 (Spring 2022); 29.2 (Fall 2022)

    EDITORS: Lydia Mattice Brandt and Michael J. Chiarappa
    REVIEW EDITOR: Rachel Leibowitz

Buildings & Landscapes: Journal of the Vernacular Architecture Forum 30.1/2 (Spring/Fall 2023)

    EDITORS: Lydia Mattice Brandt and Michael J. Chiarappa
    EDITOR DESIGNATE: Margaret M. Grubiak
    REVIEW EDITORS: Rachel Leibowitz and Amanda C. Roth Clark

Buildings & Landscapes: Journal of the Vernacular Architecture Forum 31.1 (Spring 2024)

    EDITORS: Michael J. Chiarappa and Margaret M. Grubiak
    REVIEW EDITOR: Amanda C. Roth Clark

UNIVERSITY OF MINNESOTA PRESS

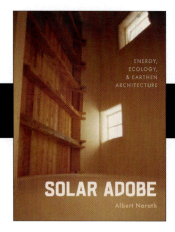  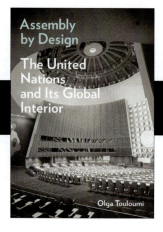 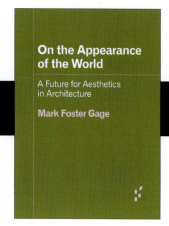

Solar Adobe
Energy, Ecology, and Earthen Architecture
Albert Narath

"Helps us recognize . . . that the seeming innovations of architecture in the twentieth century were also oppressions. As we collectively turn to these practices and materials again, Albert Narath's narrative is both instructive and inspirational." —**Daniel A. Barber**, author of *Modern Architecture and Climate: Design before Air Conditioning*

$32.95 paperback | 304 pages | 56 images

Architecture against Democracy
Histories of the Nationalist International
Reinhold Martin and Claire Zimmerman, editors

From the early nineteenth century to the present, examining architecture's foundational role in the repression of democracy

$35.00 paperback | 392 pages | 76 images

Horror in Architecture
The Reanimated Edition
Joshua Comaroff and Ong Ker-Shing

"Deeply researched, packed with detail, and bold in scope and imagination." —**Achille Mbembe**, philosopher, author of *On the Postcolony*

$24.95 paperback | 272 pages | 142 images

Assembly by Design
The United Nations and Its Global Interior
Olga Touloumi

"You'll never think about the public sphere, sound, or architecture in the same way again." —**John Durham Peters**, Yale University

$35.00 paperback | 312 pages | 119 images | September 2024
Buell Center Books in the History and Theory of American Architeture

On the Appearance of the World
A Future for Aesthetics in Architecture
Mark Foster Gage

How can architecture develop better aesthetic directions for the twenty-first-century built environment?

$10.00 paperback | 80 pages
Forerunners: Ideas First Series

The Shape of Utopia
The Architecture of Radical Reform in Nineteenth-Century America
Irene Cheng

"A deeply informed interpretation of the complex interactions between political ideals and geometric form." —**Margaret Crawford**, University of California, Berkeley

$35.00 paperback | 360 pages | 140 images
Buell Center Books in the History and Theory of American Architecture Series

University of Minnesota Press • 800-621-2736 • www.upress.umn.edu

NEW FROM THE **UNIVERSITY OF TEXAS PRESS**

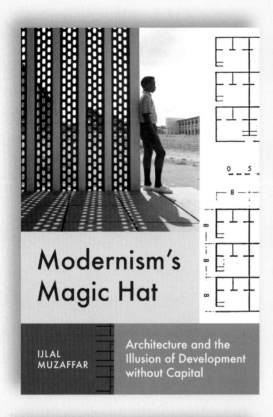
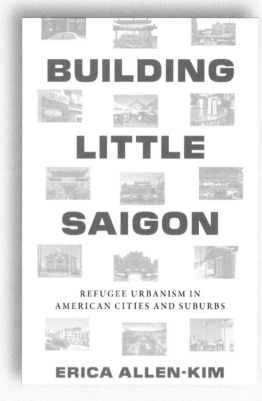
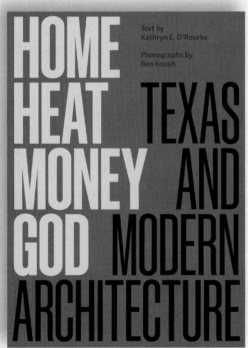

Modernism's Magic Hat
Architecture and the Illusion of Development without Capital
BY IJLAL MUZAFFAR
$39.95 *paperback*
JULY 2024

Building Little Saigon
Refugee Urbanism in American Cities and Suburbs
BY ERICA ALLEN-KIM
$39.95 *paperback*
JULY 2024

Home, Heat, Money, God
Texas and Modern Architecture
BY KATHRYN E. O'ROURKE & BEN KOUSH
$45.00 *hardcover*
MAY 2024

UNIVERSITY OF TEXAS PRESS
www.utexaspress.com | *@utexaspress*